Darren Arnold

The Pocket Essential

SPIKE LEE

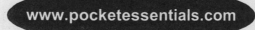

www.pocketessentials.com

First published in Great Britain 2003 by
Pocket Essentials, P O Box 394, Harpenden, Herts, AL5 1XJ, UK

Distributed in the USA by Trafalgar Square Publishing,
PO Box 257, Howe Hill Road, North Pomfret, Vermont 05053

A CIP catalogue record for this book is available from the British Library.

ISBN 1-904048-07-2

2 4 6 8 10 9 7 5 3 1

Book typeset by Wordsmith Solutions Ltd
Printed and bound by Cox & Wyman

Le.
S.

For Clare

Acknowledgements

Thanks to the following people: Helen, Richard & Denys Arnold, Helen Bernhagen, John Harrison, Dov Kornits, Andrew Leavold, John Snadden, Amanda Swinton. Also thanks to Andrew Kay for the loan of numerous DVDs and videos, and to Steve Holland for giving this project the go-ahead. Finally, thanks to Jasmine – sorry *Pi* isn't covered here, but at least *She's Gotta Have It* is in black and white!

CONTENTS

1. Spike Lee: Straight Out Of Bed-Stuy

There are few filmmakers around who produce work as controversial as Spike Lee's movies. Of the directors currently working in the US, only conspiracy theorist-elect Oliver Stone and agent provocateur Gregg Araki could be said to be producing work of a similarly incendiary nature to that of Lee. He's widely perceived to be a maverick, and as such has never really been trusted with the sort of budgets that some of his peers have been granted; from a purely financial viewpoint, this is perhaps a sound policy given that he's yet to make a film that grosses $50 million or more in the domestic market. A bit like the late Sam Peckinpah, Lee is more notorious than famous, and his work always causes more than a few ripples - even if such rustlings rarely translate into bona fide box office success.

Spike Lee effectively became a household name in 1992, some six years and as many movies into his feature film career, with the release of *Malcolm X*. Although the film fell short of its expected commercial success, it still managed to provide a reference point for even the most casual filmgoer. From that point on, Spike Lee became known as the guy who made *Malcolm X*, and he's since struggled to shake off the shadow of both the movie and the event that was the film's release. He's also never had a film that's replicated the box office success of that epic (his second most successful film is a documentary, *The Original Kings Of Comedy*, and ironically this is virtually the only film in the Lee canon that could be - and was - sold without emphasis on the Lee angle).

Although he's still firmly on the map (despite a major lull in the mid-1990s) and will probably never be reduced to working simply for food, it must be a little frustrating for Spike Lee to see how other, lesser filmmakers have progressed while he's never managed to get to the next level as far as Hollywood is concerned. And while Lee no doubt isn't all that fussed about commercial success, it nonetheless exists as a commodity that can help greatly when trying to get that all-important green light for a big budget movie. While Lee is presumably happy to whittle away on small to medium-budget films where he can retain creative autonomy, the lack of A-list clout must rankle when it comes to failing to get the money together for a project such as his much touted (and highly cherished) Jackie Robinson biopic - especially knowing that there was a time in the early 1990s when such a film would most likely have been funded. As Alan Rickman's Professor Snape hisses in *Harry Potter And The Philosopher's Stone* (2001), 'clearly, fame isn't everything.'

Shelton Jackson Lee was born in Atlanta, Georgia, on 20 March 1957. His father was musician, while his mother worked as a schoolteacher. While Spike (a nickname Shelton's mum came up with) was still young, the Lee family moved to Brooklyn, New York. Opting to go to a non-fee paying school (his mother taught at a private institution where Spike would have stood a good chance of gaining a place), he then attended Morehouse College in the city of his birth. This institution had a special significance for Spike, as both his father and grandfather had spent their college days there. While at Morehouse, Lee gained an increasing interest in cinema, and eventually decided that he wanted to make his own films.

1977 was something of a crunch year in both Spike's life and career. His mother died suddenly, which understandably had a profound effect on Spike, his father and his siblings, and in the same year he had a go at putting a short film together (*Last Hustle In Brooklyn*). He subsequently enrolled on a film course at New York University (NYU), and his first year brought about the piece of work responsible for the beginning of his gradual climb in the film world - *The Answer*. This short could have killed his career there and then (more on this in a bit), but he went on to direct the more ambitious *Joe's Bed-Stuy Barbershop: We Cut Heads*. The 45-minute film exceeded all expectations, and picked up the Student Academy Award as well as the Bronze Leopard at the Locarno Film Festival. Then, after a period resting on his laurels (but with very little income) and one significant false start, he completed his debut feature, *She's Gotta Have It*, which was released in 1986 and went on to become something of a cult classic.

From that point on, Spike has never had too much difficulty when it comes to getting his films (or 'joints,' as he prefers to call them) made. Certainly, and as we've already mentioned (and we'll cover in more detail later on), there have been problems with the funding of specific movies (such as *Malcolm X* and his Jackie Robinson biopic), but Spike has never been a director who has struggled to find work. He's a name director, and like

Spielberg, Scorsese, Allen, Coppola and a whole host of others you might care to mention, his name is usually seen as the key factor in marketing the films he has directed.

Themes

It doesn't take long for a viewer to start to pick up on the themes inherent in Spike Lee's body of work. In fact, you could probably pick any two of his films at random and spot some common ground. Of course, many people think that because many of his films are 'black' that that's the only common thread that runs through them, when in fact there are a multitude of areas that tie in across the spectrum of his work.

New York: Around two thirds of Spike Lee's feature films have been set in New York City. Many of these films have used Brooklyn as the key setting, although he's ventured outside of the borough with the likes of the predominantly Bronx-set *Summer Of Sam*. Brooklyn is where Spike grew up, so by using it in such a prominent way in his work it's clear that he's writing about (and filming) what he knows.

Wannabes: In several of Spike's films there are blacks who appear to be attempting to edge away from their African-American origins. This alludes to wanting to be white, or at the very least wanting to be something other than black. The most obvious examples of such characters are the 'wannabes' in *School Daze*, but there's also *Crooklyn*'s Aunt Song and *Bamboozled*'s Pierre Delacroix, to name just two others. Through his depiction of the 'wannabe,' Spike is pointing to an element in the black community that can be as harmful as any outside factors, and unsurprisingly those who appear to shy away from their roots are portrayed in none too favourable a light.

Family: The strong family unit figures prominently in many of Lee's films. Even if the film itself doesn't feature a stable family environment, such a state is often presented as being desirable. This theme really started to emerge in *Mo' Better Blues* and was elaborated on in *Jungle Fever*. Other works, including *Crooklyn*, *He Got Game* and *Clockers,* have also contained elements that make no secret of Lee's endorsement of the importance of family. Although you get the impression that Spike would ideally like

9

'family' to mean mum, dad and children (as featured in *Crooklyn*, *Jungle Fever* and *Mo' Better Blues*), the job of the single parent is given due time and consideration. The Jeeters in *Clockers* and the Shuttlesworths in *He Got Game* point to how one parent still has a massive influence on their children. And although *Crooklyn* and *He Got Game* both see the death of the mother as a dreadful blow to the stability of the family, there's a distinctly hopeful feeling that these family units can still survive such a setback. This is something that must come from Lee's heart, given the impact that his own mother's untimely death had on him and the rest of his family.

Community: Although it's not a theme that receives the same priority as the more immediate familial concerns outlined above, an emphasis on the importance of community is to be found in many of Lee's works. Community means a number of things in Spike Lee films - there's the campus community in *School Daze*, the Bed-Stuy community in *Do The Right Thing*, and the real-life members in the community of Birmingham in *4 Little Girls*. In broader terms, the African-American and Italian-American communities are represented in some way in the vast majority of Lee films.

Although community is seen as being important, Spike recognises the drawbacks that can be inherent in close-knit communities - think of how the respective communities/families respond to the news of a mixed-race relationship in *Jungle Fever*, or how an insular section of the Bronx's Italian-American community cooks up a fanciful scheme that gets an innocent 'outsider' into trouble in *Summer Of Sam*. Similarly, the community in *Clockers* is a far cry from the warm neighbourhood of *Crooklyn*, and in the former we're shown how a community suffers when drugs, guns and crime are at the forefront.

Tension: Where would Spike's films be without tension? From the unpleasant atmosphere around Nola's dinner table in *She's Gotta Have It* through the whole of New York City reaching (almost literally) boiling point in *Summer Of Sam*, many Lee films rely on tension for much of their mood. Spike is maybe interested in tension as it tends to be the forerunner of change, and many of his works examine how positive change - for the black community or otherwise - can be implemented.

Sports: Baseball and basketball figure prominently in much of Lee's work. If it's not actual sports sequences (such as in *He Got Game* and *Sum-*

mer Of Sam), then there are often heated conversations to be found regarding the topic (such as in *She's Gotta Have It* and *Do The Right Thing*). More on sport in Lee's films can be found later on in this book.

Violence: In Spike's films, violence can more often than not be seen as a direct result of tension (detailed above), and is one of the less positive ways in which tensions are resolved. Different Lee films contain different sorts of violence, but almost all of his films have some violent scenes. Not many people would immediately think of *She's Gotta Have It* as being such a film, but it nonetheless contains a nasty rape scene. *Do The Right Thing* explodes in the last reel, and *Mo' Better Blues* contains a juddering (but inarguably exciting) scene where two of the main characters are thrashed by thugs. *Jungle Fever* and *Summer Of Sam* both feature bloodthirsty mobs beating innocent men that were up until recently close friends with their attackers, and - perhaps most contentious of all - there's a live broadcast killing in *Bamboozled*.

In a different way, *Malcolm X* is a film where violence plays an important part, as the title character has often been put under the microscope with regard to his attitude(s) concerning violence. And last and by no means least, there's the awful real-life bombing that is the main focus of Lee's documentary *4 Little Girls*.

Violence, as Spike would almost undoubtedly agree, certainly isn't pretty, but in his films it does serve a purpose as an agent of change. For better or worse, things are never the same once a violent act has occurred - they may reach a sort of plenitude, but things definitely aren't what they were before.

Women: An oft-criticised aspect of Spike's work (particularly his early films) has been the way in which he's portrayed female characters. Despite his debut film boasting a female in the film's starring role, its message was a little unclear - Nola is supposed to be sexually liberated, but in the end she gets raped by one of the three men in her life. Many of his subsequent films were seen as being male-heavy, and even the prominently-billed Angela Bassett wasn't given too much to work with in *Malcolm X*. In other films - such as *Jungle Fever* and *Mo' Better Blues* - there was more than a hint of misogyny as female characters were given pretty shabby treatment by the males in these stories.

11

Spike appeared to set about rectifying this situation with *Crooklyn*, a film dominated by a mother and daughter, which shifted the emphasis right away from what audiences had come to know as the typical Lee world. This new-found outlook proved to be little more than a false dawn. Although he went on to make *Girl 6*, which, like Lee's debut, featured a central female character, this film was grabbing for air amidst almost exclusively male-dominated works such as *Clockers* and *Get On The Bus*. Even in *Girl 6*, the eponymous character had to show her breasts to Quentin Tarantino's leering director, which causes the viewer to examine who it is who actually wants the girl to expose herself - the real or the fictional filmmaker?

He Got Game does little in the way of presenting positive female characters - main character Jesus is warned off women (cue shots of a busty woman in *flagrante delicto*), while his girlfriend plots behind his back. There's also a battered prostitute who's under the thumb of her evil pimp.

Summer Of Sam was perhaps the film that proved that Spike's *Crooklyn* state of mind was well behind him - John Leguizamo's misogynistic Vinny cheats on his sweet wife while referring to his best friend's girl as 'a whore.' Although the two central female performances are good, the characters are hardly positive female types - Vinny's wife is little more than a cuckold (albeit one who ultimately gets wise), while the other character is coerced into acting in porn films by her boyfriend. Not exactly girl power.

Education: The value Spike places on education is apparent in his work. The most obvious way in which education is featured is through the college setting of *School Daze*, but there are several other examples where the importance of learning surfaces. In *Jungle Fever* shop worker Paulie is interested in attending college, and discusses this with one of his customers. *He Got Game* focuses on young basketball player Jesus' choice of university, and although he's obviously going to college on a sports scholarship it's clear that he's also being presented with a valuable opportunity to learn. In *Crooklyn* the mother is a schoolteacher who's seen as having a vital job to do - possibly something that was passed down to Spike from his own teacher mother. *Clockers* sees the value that a mother places on her child's education; the boy is a bright pupil, and it's obvious that the mother sees his academic prowess as the way in which he'll be able to avoid slipping into a life of crime like so many other boys in the neighbourhood. In *Girl 6* the main character sets about attending acting classes in order that she might escape from the treadmill of unsatisfying jobs that she's found herself working in, and her goals are seen as being worthwhile. In all these cases, education is seen as an important tool for progression in life - for people in general, and blacks in particular. Although not education in the formal sense, what *Malcolm X*'s title character learns in prison serves him well, and helps him to focus on where he and his ancestors have been, who he is, and where he's going.

Police: On the whole the law hasn't been given too much to be proud of in Spike's films. As early on as *Do The Right Thing* we had a situation where bull-headed officers strangled an unarmed man to death. This was followed up by a sequence in *Jungle Fever* where armed police leapt on a black man who was having a mock fight with his white girlfriend, and in *Get On The Bus* there was a scene where state troopers intimidated a busload of black men. However, without a doubt the most damning indictment of the police in a Spike film comes not with Lee's interpretations of law enforcement officials, but rather actual footage of transgressive officers: *Malcolm X* opened with the real-life beating of Los Angeles motorist Rodney King, and these images are far more damaging than anything any filmmaker - Lee included - has to say about the police.

The depiction of the police isn't entirely unfavourable, however, and in *Clockers* the two white detectives are portrayed in a sympathetic manner - they're seen as flawed characters, but ones who have a difficult job to do. In the same film, the local police officer is also painted as being an essentially decent person, yet one who's not above using excessive force at times.

In *Summer Of Sam* there's a couple of detectives who are seen as being fairly harmless and ineffective; also, the Italian-American detective appears to be a couple of steps away from being in the hands of the mob, and there are heavy allusions to a childhood spent running errands for a local crime boss. Interestingly, Lee has paired the Italian-American policeman with an African-American partner, and the black detective is understandably offended at the local gangsters' racially loaded remarks. Although these two are not as heavy-handed and cynical as the pair in *Clockers*, they're nonetheless seen as being not particularly useful. On the other hand, perhaps that's just a symptom of the horrendous job that they've got on their hands.

After all, with lootings, killings and blackouts happening all over New York, who'd have been an NYC cop in '77?

Although outside of the actual police force but sticking with the judicial theme, *He Got Game* features a prison governor who is prepared to make an underhand deal with an inmate yet may well renege on his promise on the grounds of a technicality; also, the fact that a black man is serving what appears to be a very harsh sentence for his crime seems to be an indictment of the way in which blacks are discriminated against in the US legal system.

Italian-Americans: Spike's depictions of Italian-Americans has often come into criticism from those who feel that he's all too often provided a stereotypical view of the community. Sure, Spike's Italian-Americans often tend to be bully boys who love their mums yet have no qualms in dishing out beatings for little or no reason. But they are also seen to be almost neurotically Catholic, and are forever fearful of getting on the wrong side of God. Throw in the depiction of Italian-American women as existing for no reason other than to wash, cook and clean for the men, and you can perhaps see where these protestations come from.

Some of Spike's typical Italian-Americans: *Summer Of Sam*'s Vinny, who has a real thing for extra-marital sex yet constantly fears God's thunderbolt (the same film also features a mob boss called - oh yes - Luigi); *Do The Right Thing*'s Sal, who loves Italian-American actors and runs a - wait for it - pizzeria; *Jungle Fever*'s Lou and Mike, two tyrannical patriarchs who constantly remind their offspring of the paragons of virtue known as 'your mother'; *Clockers*' Larry Mazilli, a weasel-like detective whose mistrust of blacks is obvious; and so on.

Of course, it can be argued that stereotypes come about as a result of observing behavioural patterns, and perhaps in many ways Spike (as a New Yorker) is drawing from his own experiences of Italian-Americans. As Spike himself is African-American, his experience of Italian-Americans is quite obviously limited, and although his view of the Italian-American community has at times been hackneyed it would be a pretty dull cinematic world if directors weren't allowed to represent people of different ethnic backgrounds to their own.

As to why Spike has often chosen to throw Italian-Americans into his films instead of, say, the Spanish or Irish communities, Spike has said that he feels that those other communities are not as strong as they once were, whereas Italian neighbourhoods are still very common across New York City (and other parts of the US).

Inter-racial relationships: Black/white relationships feature in several of Spike's films, and in general terms those involved in such relationships don't have that easy a time of it. The most prominent inter-racial affair features in *Jungle Fever*, where a black architect falls for his white secretary, but there are other occasions. In fact there is another instance in the same film, where a white shop worker falls for a black customer and is subsequently given a good thrashing for his progressive thinking. In *Do The Right Thing* we see Italian-American Sal pursuing the sister of his black delivery boy, only to be warned off (it's not entirely clear if this is on the grounds of race, or simply because the employee doesn't like the idea of his boss pawing his sister). In *Mo' Better Blues* one of the characters is teased about having a relationship with a white girl, and in *Malcolm X* the title character is seen to have a Caucasian girlfriend. In both films, however, the protagonists end up in intra-racial relationships.

While none of this can really be described as hopeful, perhaps it's more a case of Spike drawing what he sees as being the difficulties that are presented to people who are in such relationships.

History: Although he's essentially a director who's taken to chronicling modern-day America, Spike's films often remind the audience of times past, and particularly the roles that African-Americans (such as Malcolm X) have played in America's history. This is sometimes presented in a general way (the 'coons' in *Bamboozled* are representative of both historical attitudes and present-day stereotyping), and African-Americans are often shown to have been on the back foot as far as the pecking order in the US is concerned.

Outside of the actual scenes of Spike's films, the credits sequences in his films remind us of a significant historical episode regarding blacks in America: Spike's production company is named '40 Acres & A Mule Filmworks' - a title which refers to broken promises that were made to blacks following emancipation in the late 19th century.

Hair: In a number of Spike's films peoples' differing hairstyles provide talking points. In *School Daze* the two opposing factions in the college are partly defined by their different types of hair, and in *Malcolm X* we see the title character undergo the painful-looking process known as 'conking' (where kinked hair is straightened using congolene). In *Crooklyn* the straightness/kinkiness of hair becomes an issue when a young girl stays with her stuck-up aunt, and in *Summer Of Sam* we get a character who has changed his hairstyle to a Mohawk - a move which arouses great suspicion among his peers. In the same film, many women sport blonde wigs as they perceive this to be a cunning decoy that'll help them outwit the apparently brunette-targeting serial killer.

Style

Although Spike Lee has worked across all film formats (ranging from Super 8 to Digital Video) and has made a number of films that possess a different look and feel, there are nonetheless a number of common areas that shine through in many of his films.

Credits: A Spike Lee joint usually provides something to talk about when it comes to the title sequence. Perhaps the best early example of an innovative opening credits sequence comes with *Do The Right Thing*, where a body-popping Rosie Perez throws shapes to the strains of Public Enemy's anthemic *Fight The Power*. *Jungle Fever* has an equally brilliant title sequence, in which the cast and crew's names are presented in the style of a variety of road signs and street names. *Malcolm X*, of course, has the most notorious opening sequence of all of Spike's films, and includes footage of a burning US flag and the beating of Rodney King. Despite any objections that people may have regarding the content of this sequence, there can be no denying both the technical achievement and the visceral power of the piece. *He Got Game* also sports an impressive credits sequence, detailed in the 'montage' section below.

Two of Spike's most recent films - *Bamboozled* and *Summer Of Sam* - have gone the opposite way of some of his earlier work by having no opening credits whatsoever. Still, they're notable through their absence, and provide yet another talking point for viewers of Lee films.

Montage: Spike has often been fond of introducing montage sequences into his movies, and this is usually something that he's able to do quite effectively. Perhaps the most famous example of this technique comes with the 'racial slur montage' (Spike's own description) that is to be found in *Do The Right Thing*. With its rapid-fire delivery of dialogue and clever device of not letting us know who in particular the slurs are aimed at (presumably everyone in the respective communities), this sequence has a real intensity. Some audiences laugh, others wince, but it's a stretch of film that always gets a reaction.

A more sober example of Lee's use of montage comes at the end of *Bamboozled*, where we're shown an elongated collection of clips highlighting black stereotyping (and blatant racism) in the movies and TV. Whether it's seeing Judy Garland and Bugs Bunny in blackface, or catching a few moments from the inspiration for one of Spike's student films, *Birth of a Nation* (1915), this is an incredibly affecting sequence.

There are several other examples where Spike uses montage to real emotional effect, and one of these is a terrible scene in *Clockers* where young anti-hero Strike is seen playing with his train set, before the scene is interspersed with images of crackheads doing what they do. On a more positive note, Spike's montage of young people (both black and white) playing basketball that opens *He Got Game* is a beautiful piece of filmmaking, and the close of the same film sees Spike capture the spirit of Coney Island with numerous shots of the rides and attractions to be found in the world-famous Astroland.

However, by far the best example of montage in a Spike Lee film is to be found in *Summer Of Sam*, and the big show stopping moment comes with a series of shots of the film's characters accompanied by The Who's classic track *Baba O'Riley*. With its refrain of 'teenage wasteland,' this sequence may not be the most subtle but there can be little doubting the suitability of this Pete Townshend track in providing a soundtrack to a sequence replete with killings, drug abuse and sex acts.

Mugging: More than one of Spike's films features characters speaking straight to camera, and in *She's Gotta Have It* the mugging is at its worst. We have to sit through Nola and her three men talking straight at us as we hear them introduce their respective sides of the love square. It doesn't work, but at least Spike managed this technique to a higher standard by the time he got to *Do The Right Thing*; the aforementioned sequence where numerous characters (headed by Lee's own Mookie) reel off a succession of racial slurs is highly effective. *He Got Game* features the members of a basketball team all taking their turn to say their piece to the camera as they wax lyrical about the joys of the game, and in *Summer Of Sam* journalist Jimmy Breslin opens (and closes) the picture with a spiel about New York City; in the same film even Spike gets to weigh in with his own bit of mugging to the camera with his cameo as a TV reporter.

Although straight to camera dialogue can often be a jarring experience for the viewer, it's something that Spike has persisted with. Perhaps the reason that it is a feature of quite a few of his films is simply because he knows that it can make audiences uncomfortable, and Spike Lee is usually pretty happy when he's turning his audience on the spit.

Music: Music has played an important part in Spike Lee's films, and for the most part that music has been rooted in the Jazz tradition: Spike's father Bill scored all of his son's films up to and including *Mo' Better Blues*, while trumpeter Terence Blanchard came in from *Jungle Fever* onwards. There have been a couple of other people who've worked on the music for Lee films since *Jungle Fever* - such as Prince on *Girl 6* and Aaron Copland on *He Got Game* - but Blanchard has really been Lee's composer of choice for well over ten years.

Of course, there are other musical artists whose work is featured in Lee films, particularly as far as songs are concerned. Stevie Wonder's work can be heard in *School Daze*, *Jungle Fever* and *Bamboozled*, while Bruce Hornsby has contributed songs to both *Clockers* and *Bamboozled*. Spike's Public Enemy buddies helped open *Do The Right Thing* with their explosive *Fight The Power* (Lee reciprocated by directing the music video for the song), and nearly a decade later the same group penned the songs for *He Got Game*. Perhaps reflective of the first Spike film to have a mainly white cast, The Who's back catalogue was plundered for the soundtrack of *Summer Of Sam*.

Film Stock: One thing that seems to impress and irritate viewers in roughly equal measure is Spike's fondness of fiddling around with the film stock during his movies. The earliest example of this comes with the colour birthday sequence in the otherwise entirely black and white *She's Gotta Have It*, and it proves to be an effective if somewhat crude device on that occasion. Since then, Spike has become rather more adept at such tricks, although he has at times been in real danger of overplaying his hand when it comes to employing this technique. For example, *Get On The Bus* features a number of changes in film stock, and, given that this film's supposed to play pretty much like a documentary, you'd think that Spike wouldn't want people to be distracted from the story in any way. And in *Crooklyn* he uses an anamorphic lens for certain scenes, which does little other than leave the viewer scratching their head as they search for a perceptible point to this tactic.

There are times when such a calculation has paid off - the 16mm inserts that pop up in the Digital Video feature *Bamboozled* perform an important task in presenting the viewer with a show within a film, and the fantasy sequences in *Girl 6* are amusingly filmed in an oversaturated manner that's far removed from the majority of the movie. Also, *Clockers* cleverly employs different stocks for different areas of the city, and at times the film would pass for a documentary about life in the projects. The whole of *Summer Of Sam* is shot on a grainy stock that has an appropriately lurid '70s feel; the scenes with David Berkowitz and at the infamous Plato's Retreat seem to be even more washed-out that the rest of the film, while the *Baba O'Riley* sequence appears to feature a squeezing technique that's the opposite of the anamorphic parts of *Crooklyn*.

Cinematography: Almost all of Spike Lee's films feature sterling camerawork. There are only a couple of films where the photography doesn't really make the grade, and one of those is the Arthur Jafa-shot *Crooklyn*. As obvious a statement as it sounds, different skin colours require different treatment from a cinematographer, and as most of Spike's films have featured mainly black actors it was obviously important that the director of photography (DoP) got it right. Up to and including *Malcolm X*, Lee's films were shot by Ernest Dickerson, who's not only one of the best cinematographers in recent times but also someone who knows exactly how to photograph black faces; his use of light remains virtually unparalleled in Nineties cinema. Once Dickerson departed to pursue a directorial career, Spike's films didn't look quite as grand when photographed by Malik Hassan Sayeed (excepting *He Got Game*), Elliot Davis and the aforementioned Jafa, but recently he seems to have found a worthy DoP in Ellen Kuras, whose work on *4 Little Girls*, *Summer Of Sam* and *Bamboozled* has brought a striking visual quality back to Lee's films that was absent in the likes of *Girl 6* and *Get On The Bus*.

Having now read a bit about what constitutes a Spike Lee film, it should be evident that much of his work carries the weight of controversy; in addition to the questions that certain quarters have raised regarding the representations of Italian-Americans and women, he's also been accused of homophobia and anti-Semitism. However, it would be less than true to state that the interest in Spike Lee's films hasn't been at least partly due to the controversial nature of much of his work; he's a director who, like Ken Russell and the aforementioned Sam Peckinpah, has no qualms about spicing up his work with a little bit of shock value. He has points to make and axes to grind, after all, and he's not scared to employ a tactic if he knows that it'll gain a bit more coverage for his movie.

That said, there's a real danger - particularly to newcomers to Lee's work - that Spike's movies can be simply dismissed as containing nothing other than angry, empty rhetoric. The contentious streak that runs through nearly every one of his feature films has acted as a double-edged sword - his films might get noticed, but perhaps the relatively poor box office figures are reflective of audiences who feel that there is little more to a Spike movie than a forced, gimmicky controversy. The opening sequence of *Malcolm X*, for example, proved to be such a talking point to the extent that it effectively dwarfed the rich content of the film itself.

There are plenty of good reasons to watch Spike Lee films, although, and as the analyses of the individual films will indicate, his body of work can't really be described as a discrete whole: there are some great movies and some very poor movies in his filmography. However, more often than not you'll be presented with strong performances and the work of superior technicians, and the bulk of his work is visually interesting (regardless of how the narrative grabs you). Beyond his initial brace of feature films, his movies have always been of a high technical standard and he's never been afraid to employ an experimental approach when filming certain segments of his features.

Above all else, however, Spike's films are always worth a look as the director's personality always comes through in his work; while watching one of his films you can really feel that this is the work of a guy who is bursting with things to say and can't wait to stick his ideas up there on the screen. Some of it may be bombastic, some of it might fail, but with a Spike Lee film you're pretty much guaranteed an interesting ride that's a clever antidote to the most of the cinema that's currently on offer.

2. Early Work

Like all filmmakers, Spike Lee had to start somewhere, and once he'd caught the bug it was only a matter of time before he got his hands on a camera and started to fashion his own short works. Although Spike's initial efforts met with wildly varying degrees of success (come to think of it, much like his later full-length features), they provided him with a reasonable range of experience that would stand him in good stead for when he'd get to the stage where he was able to make features.

Last Hustle In Brooklyn (1977)

As the idea of becoming a filmmaker began to sink into Spike's mind, he spent the summer of '77 wandering around New York with a Super 8 camera. From the resulting footage he pieced together a film that captured part of the spirit of that summer, replete with street parties and people grooving to Van McCoy's disco anthem *The Hustle*. The film's title was an amalgam of that famous '70s number and Hubert Selby Jr.'s notorious New York-set novel *Last Exit To Brooklyn*.

The Answer (1980)

A ten-minute effort that attempted to redo D. W. Griffith's controversial epic *Birth Of A Nation*. This was Spike's first-year film for his NYU course, and its jibes at screen legend Griffith did little to please Spike's university tutors. Using the device of having a black screenwriter attempt to rewrite to Griffith film, *The Answer* was seen as a daring experiment - so daring, in fact, that it almost got its director booted out of NYU.

Sarah (1981)

After the bold nature of *The Answer*, Spike played it safe with this effort. Concentrating on Thanksgiving in Harlem, little is really known about this film and it doesn't pop up too often in filmographies of the director.

Joe's Bed-Stuy Barbershop: We Cut Heads (1984)

Lee's much talked about thesis film, set against the backdrop of Brooklyn's Bedford-Stuyvesant neighbourhood - an area which would subsequently serve as the setting for *Do The Right Thing*. Barber Joe is iced by a local hood, and Zack Homer (Monty Ross) takes over the vacant salon. All Zack wants to do is run a legit barbershop, but things get sticky when the hood appears and proposes a plan to improve business for the sparsely patronised shop.

By winning the Student Academy Award, *Joe's Bed-Stuy Barbershop* appeared to give Spike's career a real shot in the arm. He landed representation through the well-known William Morris Agency, who assured him all he had to do was wait by the phone. When it didn't ring, he got a job in film distribution to help pay the bills, and then set about writing and prepping a feature...

The Messenger (1984; unfinished)

Intended to be Spike's first feature, *The Messenger* was a partly autobiographical story about a bike courier. With the script together and a crew assembled, *The Messenger* went into six weeks of pre-production; it all fell through, however, when the producer failed to deliver the promised funds.

3. The Truth, Ruth

After the abortive attempt at feature making that was *The Messenger*, Spike was understandably some way short of being Mr. Popular. He and his crew had spent the summer on all the preliminary work, and when the finance for the film didn't come through everyone involved was left disappointed. Having wasted the time of a lot of people, Spike found himself in a very difficult situation, and thus scaled down his ambitions for his first feature film. As we all know, when that first film actually materialised in the form of *She's Gotta Have It*, Spike was able to work in *The Messenger*'s bike courier angle with the character of Mars Blackmon.

Spike's ideas about making *She's Gotta Have It* stand as a good example to many a budding filmmaker. He wasn't shooting for the moon, but rather wanted to make a film that could be photographed in a few days with just a handful of cast and crew. Further to that, he intended to do virtually everything on location, which not only minimised costs but also provided an inbuilt authenticity that shoestring studio productions often lack.

She's Gotta Have It (1986)

Cast: Tracy Camilla Johns (Nola), Spike Lee (Mars), Tommy Redmond Hicks (Jamie), John Canada Terrell (Greer), Joie Lee (Clorinda), Pamm Jackson (Female Walk On), Bill Lee (Sonny), Ernest Dickerson (Dog 8), Monty Ross (Dog 1), Raye Dowell (Opal).

Crew: Writer/Producer/Director/Editor Spike Lee, Associate Producer Pamm Jackson, Sound Designer Barry Alexander Brown, Music Bill Lee, Production Designer Wynn Thomas, Cinematography Ernest Dickerson, Production Supervisor Monty Ross, Costume Design John Michael Reefer.

Story: Brooklyn layout artist Nola Darling juggles the attentions of three different lovers. There's the seemingly sensitive Jamie, vain male model Greer and clownish bike messenger Mars. Nola likes the positive aspects of each of the men, but finds that no single one of them possesses all the qualities she looks for; therefore, she can't choose just one of them. Wondering if there's something wrong with her, Nola sees a sex therapist, which does little to help her predicament.

Having also attracted the attentions of lesbian Opal, Nola realises that she has to take control and start making some decisions in her life. Nola is date-raped by Jamie, and realises that he sees her as a trophy to be possessed. Nola concludes that she's simply not a one-man woman.

Comment: She's Gotta Have It neatly inverts the familiar scenario of a male who keeps several girlfriends on the go at once - think of it as being something like *Alfie* (1966) through the looking glass. Unlike the title character in *Alfie*, Nola is a bit more honest about her multiple sexual relationships, and Mars, Jamie and Greer are each aware that they're not Nola's one and only. Just like *Alfie*, however, the film features direct to camera monologues, which are perhaps designed to lend authenticity but if anything distance the viewer from the film.

With *She's Gotta Have It*, Spike Lee appears to be commenting on female sexuality, although Nola is a fairly ambiguous character - are we supposed to applaud this headstrong woman, or frown upon her fickleness? Most viewers may be undecided about Nola until late on in the film, where the unpleasant date-rape scene makes Nola an object of viewer sympathy. Ultimately, though, *She's Gotta Have It* is a pretty slight tale that lacks the substance of Lee's best work. And despite the film's title and reputation, there isn't that much sex in the film - subsequent works such as *He Got Game* and *Summer Of Sam* feature far more sex than can be glimpsed here.

Made for a paltry $175,000, *She's Gotta Have It* might not have been anything close to a masterpiece, but its commercial success put Spike Lee firmly on the map. Made on location with a small cast, the film was knocked out in around two weeks, and Spike edited the footage in his own apartment. A debt-ridden Lee managed to get the final print together, Island Pictures picked up the distribution rights, and the film went on to make more than $7 million at the US box office. And while *She's Gotta Have It* can only really be described as a qualified success, it nonetheless served its purpose in giving Lee a foothold in the filmmaking world. Many fans and critics tend to get very sentimental when recalling an established filmmaker's first feature, and *She's Gotta Have It* has received a lot of praise

Mission College is clearly meant to be a microcosm of black America, and it'd be naïve to think that Dap's call to 'wake up' is meant only for ears within the campus grounds.

School Daze also touches upon other areas - albeit it in an almost completely ham-fisted manner - such as the US's policy regarding South Africa, which may seem less relevant in the present day but of course was of real significance back in the time of apartheid and pre-Mandela power. It seems incredulous that an all black college should be investing in the South Africa of 1988, and this is presumably put in there to show us another way in which blacks are contributing to their own lack of advancement; just as in-fighting is hurting the black community, the sending of money to a country known for its ill treatment of blacks is hardly going to help anyone - other than those concerned with racial oppression. (NB: Spike Lee has always had a clause in his contracts stating that his films can't be distributed in South Africa.)

Although with *School Daze* Lee undeniably has some important things to say, the film is so overblown that ultimately it's hard to take too much from it. The points it makes are effectively smothered by a combination of unconvincing face-offs between one-dimensional characters and a barrage of jarring musical numbers. It seems as if Lee is caught between making something that can exist simply on its own terms and actually creating a work that has some thematic resonance, and *School Daze* is neither a good yarn nor a credible analogy for black America. The scenario of racial problems on a college campus was dealt with in a far more effective manner in another Laurence Fishburne movie: John Singleton's *Higher Learning* (1994).

However, despite its myriad flaws there is one sequence in the film that rises way above anything else on display here (or, for that matter, in *She's Gotta Have It*) - a song and dance number entitled *Straight And Nappy* (the title refers to the different types of hair that provide the basis for much of the film's intra-racial sniping). In this superbly devised segment, the 'jigaboo' girls take the opportunity to hurl numerous insults at their 'wannabe' opposite numbers, and vice versa. There's something extremely impressive about this pulsating sequence, and its burning brilliance seems to come from nowhere. Sadly, it's the only real moment where Lee's obvious wit and intelligence shine through, and plays almost as if it has been inserted from another work altogether.

Unlike *She's Gotta Have It*, *School Daze* is a highly ambitious work. However, it seems to be a case where Lee was trying to run before he could walk, and he would almost undoubtedly have been better off had he made something on a scale similar to that of his first film. While *She's Gotta Have It* was no *Citizen Kane* (1941) it did possess a glimmer of promise, which no doubt could have been built upon had Spike not been let off the leash for *School Daze*. The film feels out of control, and looks like the work of a director who's unleashed a Frankenstein's monster that he has no idea of how to tame.

Anyway, the dollar rules, and regardless of its quality *School Daze* made twice as much money as *She's Gotta Have It*. Spike's career was on the up.

Spike's Stock: School Daze marked the beginning of Spike's long associations with costume designer Ruth E Carter and production designer Wynn Thomas. Barry Alexander Brown edited his first movie for Lee, while Monty Ross acted as co-producer for the first time.

Acting-wise, *School Daze* was the first Lee film to feature Samuel L Jackson, Bill Nunn, Giancarlo Esposito and Ossie Davis. Spike's brother Cinqué also appears.

Trivia: School Daze featured a couple of performers who'd obviously caught the directing bug - James Bond III went on to direct *Def By Temptation* (1990), while Kasi Lemmons made the acclaimed *Eve's Bayou* (1997). Incidentally, both films starred *School Daze*'s Samuel L Jackson.

Part of *School Daze* was filmed at Atlanta's Morehouse College - Spike's alma mater.

Verdict: Aiming far higher than *She's Gotta Have It*, *School Daze* ultimately buckles under its own weight as Lee finds he's not up to the task he's set himself. A good initial concept counts for little when it's so poorly executed, and at half an hour longer than Spike's debut this film - *Straight And Nappy* aside – it is pretty hard going. 2/5.

After a clutch of shorts (which admittedly included a Student Oscar-winner) and two overwhelmingly mediocre features, it wouldn't have been too surprising if Spike Lee had gone on to churn out a couple more similarly unremarkable features before falling off the map altogether. Perhaps he was well aware that his work up to this point had been sub-standard, as Spike's next film, themes and personnel aside, was barely recognisable as being the work of the man who'd made very heavy weather of two modest features.

Do The Right Thing (1989)

Cast: Danny Aiello (Sal), Ossie Davis (Da Mayor), John Turturro (Pino), John Savage (Clifton), Spike Lee (Mookie), Bill Nunn (Radio Raheem), Ruby Dee (Mother Sister), Giancarlo Esposito (Buggin' Out), Samuel L Jackson (Mister Señor Love Daddy), Richard Edson (Vito), Frank Vincent (Charlie), Rosie Perez (Tina), Joie Lee (Jade), Martin Lawrence (Cee).

Crew: Writer/Producer/Director Spike Lee, Co-Producer Monty Ross, Line Producer Jon Kilik, Editor Barry Alexander Brown, Music Bill Lee, Production Designer Wynn Thomas, Cinematography Ernest Dickerson, Costume Design Ruth E Carter.

Story: Sal is the Italian-American owner of a pizzeria in Bedford-Stuyvesant, Brooklyn. The majority of the people in the neighbourhood are black - Sal's delivery man Mookie, local sage Da Mayor, music fanatic Radio Raheem and militant Buggin' Out are just a few of the characters that populate the area.

On one particularly hot day, tensions are beginning to rise. Buggin' Out has begun to object to the lack of black faces among the celebrity pictures that adorn the pizzeria walls, and is duly ejected by Sal. Sal is clearly enamoured with Mookie's sister, and is greatly irritated when his delivery boy warns him off.

Buggin' Out attempts to organise a boycott of the pizzeria, but no one other than Radio Raheem is interested. The two walk into Sal's, and the annoyed owner destroys Raheem's blaring radio with a baseball bat. In the ensuing fracas, the police arrive and easily overpower Buggin' Out. Raheem proves more difficult to restrain, and one of the panicked officers chokes him to death. This turns the majority of the neighbourhood against Sal, and they loot and set fire to the pizzeria.

Comment: Many critics still refer to *Do The Right Thing* as being Spike Lee's best film, and while it's a great slice of filmmaking it's not quite up there with some of his later work. And neither should it be, in logical terms - Spike was still learning his craft when he made *Do The Right Thing*, and perhaps the reason why it was so well received was because it came on the back of two relative duds. It's certainly one of Spike's better films, but you can't help thinking that the sort of person still hailing it as Spike's master-work is the sort who's never been able to see beyond *Taxi Driver* (1976) as far as Martin Scorsese is concerned, or who thinks that Stanley Kubrick's career was all downhill after *Dr Strangelove* (1963).

Do The Right Thing was really the first (but by no means the last) Lee film to deal with tensions between black and white communities. *She's Gotta Have It* was more concerned with sexuality than racial issues, and *School Daze* looked at in-fighting within the black community. The signifi-cant white characters in *Do The Right Thing* are pizzeria owner Sal, his two sons Pino and Vito, and John Savage's much-pilloried Clifton.

In many ways *Do The Right Thing* is quite an ambiguous work, as it offers little in the way of solutions to the problems that are presented throughout the course of the film. The tensions of that baking hot Saturday are only relieved once a black man has been killed and a white man's shop has been destroyed, which on the face of it doesn't really sound like an ideal way to sort out differences. This ambiguity even extends to the closing cred-its, where an anti-violence quote from Martin Luther King ('violence as a way of achieving racial justice is both impractical and immoral') sits next to Malcolm X's qualified endorsement of violence ('I don't even call it vio-lence when it's self defence - I call it intelligence.') To have these two state-ments together seems contradictory, but Lee has since commented that although the two viewpoints are very different, both are valid. Even if *Do The Right Thing* doesn't gift-wrap a solution for us, one thing Spike Lee clearly wants us all to do is to have a long, hard look at ourselves. *School Daze* ended with Larry Fishburne screaming 'wake up', and *Do The Right Thing* starts with Sam Jackson telling us to do exactly the same thing (the phrase pops up in many of Lee's films). That's a pretty clear indicator that Spike wants us to do something other than keep making the same old mis-takes in the same somnambulant manner. And if we do wake up and think about how we lead our lives, we're at least given a strong hint as to what we should actually be doing - the film's title gives us a pretty good rule of thumb, as does Da Mayor when he utters the same words in a moment of clarity. It's certainly a film to get you thinking - for example, at the close of the film you'll probably look at Sal's trashed pizzeria and feel sorry for the owner, whereas the overriding sympathy should surely go out to Radio Raheem. After all, loss of life is far more tragic than loss of property.

Although *Do The Right Thing* might not have any real suggestions for solving racial tensions, it does at least act as a cautionary tale in which we are shown how petty situations can quickly escalate into tragedy. Buggin' Out's objections to the Italian-American photos on Sal's wall appear to be the product of a man with too much time on his hands and too little common sense, and Lee is able to laugh at such a character. After all, Buggin' Out is the sort of guy who loses the plot when his new Nike trainers are accidentally scuffed by local white man Clifton - not the sort of activity a would-be world-changer should be taking part in, you'd have thought. Although something of a buffoon, Buggin' Out initiates the boycott of Sal's, and this is really the point where proceedings start to take a very grim turn. What starts as a silly complaint ultimately leads to a riot and the death of Radio Raheem, and at the end who is to blame? Is it Sal, who lost his temper with Raheem? Or is it Buggin' Out, who roped Raheem into his juvenile protest? A lot of the blame could even be said to lie with Mookie, who virtually initiates the riot by smashing Sal's window with a metal bin. It's completely open to interpretation, and the point seems to be that it's no particular person that's wholly to blame but rather the simmering tensions that exist between the communities. If it wasn't the pizzeria boycott that brought things to a head then it would have been something else - maybe not on that day, but at some point. Sal and Buggin' Out aren't really squaring up to each other because of the pictures on the pizzeria walls, but rather because of their dislike of one another on the grounds of skin colour.

There are a few rational voices in the film - local DJ and Greek chorus Mister Señor Love Daddy (armed with his incremental catchphrase, '...and that's the truth, Ruth,') and Mookie's pleasant and easy-going sister Jade, plus the frequently drunk but essentially level-headed Da Mayor and the watchful Mother Sister - but even they can't influence things for the better on that fateful Saturday. What's left for these Bed-Stuy residents will forever remain a mystery to viewers, although a fairly heated but peculiarly positive exchange between Sal and Mookie at the close of the film hints that things may return to some form of normality.

There can be no denying that *Do The Right Thing* is an important film, and it was the first film where Spike appeared to be in control of his material. The sloppiness of *She's Gotta Have It* and *School Daze* are pleasingly absent, and from as early on as the dazzling opening credits sequence it's very clear that this is a filmmaker who's really learned from his early mistakes.

Spike's Stock: Mostly returning members on the production side of things. In front of the camera, John Turturro made his first of many appearances for Spike.

Trivia: The part of Sal is said to have been written with Robert De Niro in mind.

Do The Right Thing was nominated for a best screenplay Academy Award; in the end it lost out to *Dead Poets Society* (1989). Danny Aiello was also up for an award, but missed out on the best supporting actor Oscar. Ironically, the award went to one of Lee's future collaborators - Denzel Washington.

Verdict: Do The Right Thing was infinitely better than Lee's first two films, and the leap in quality from *School Daze* to here is nothing short of remarkable. With standout performances from the whole cast, *Do The Right Thing* is one of Lee's more satisfying movies, although it does lack the polish of his very best work. 4/5.

Mo' Better Blues (1990)

Cast: Denzel Washington (Bleek Gilliam), Wesley Snipes (Shadow Henderson), Spike Lee (Giant), Samuel L Jackson (Madlock), Cynda Williams (Clarke), Joie Lee (Indigo), Ruben Blades (Petey), John Turturro (Moe), Tracy Camilla Johns (Club Patron), Flavor Flav (Impatient Movie Patron), Monty Ross (Club Patron), Nicholas Turturro (Josh), Raye Dowell (Rita).

Crew: Writer/Producer/Director Spike Lee, Co-Producer Monty Ross, Line Producer Jon Kilik, Editor Sam Pollard, Music Bill Lee, Production Designer Wynn Thomas, Cinematography Ernest Dickerson, Costume Design Ruth E. Carter.

Story: Trumpeter Bleek Gilliam plays as part of a quintet at the Beneath the Underground club. The group is managed by Giant, who is in the process of running up serious gambling debts. Bleek has two women in his life - schoolteacher Indigo and singer Clarke.

The other members of the group - led by saxophonist Shadow - tell Bleek that they want a different manager, but Bleek maintains his loyalty to Giant. Giant is under pressure to pay his gambling debts, and has already been roughed up by two thugs. Shadow has become romantically interested in Clarke, and the two begin an affair. Bleek learns of Giant's massive debts and promptly fires the manager; Giant informs Bleek of Shadow and Clarke's relationship. At the club, the two thugs take Giant outside and beat him up. Bleek tries to help, but ends up in hospital.

With Bleek's trumpet-playing days over, he settles down with Indigo. They marry and have a son.

Comment: Although *Mo' Better Blues* is longer in duration than *Do The Right Thing*, its scope is much smaller than that of its predecessor. However, despite the thematic scaling down, Spike manages to make a real mess of a picture that really should have consolidated his standing after the success of *Do The Right Thing*. It's almost as if Spike can't raise his game when he's working with material that doesn't stretch him, and thus comes something of a cropper. You can't help but feel that *Mo' Better Blues* was a project suited to an earlier, hungrier Spike - say, the one that couldn't really get to grips with the ideas in *School Daze*. By the same token, *School Daze* might have worked better had it followed *Do The Right Thing*, and Spike might been able to make something more of that film once he'd attained an extended filmmaking vocabulary.

As in *She's Gotta Have It*, *Mo' Better Blues* isn't really concerned with racial conflict - the vast majority of characters are black, but the problems that are thrown up have little to do with racial tensions. Instead, *Mo' Better Blues* is more concerned with sexuality and male-female relationships. Like *She's Gotta Have It*'s Nola, flighty trumpeter Bleek keeps more than one partner on the go and for the bulk of the film can't decide on who he should settle down with. Bleek is not a character with whom the audience can have too much sympathy, as apart from stringing two girls along he's extremely self-obsessed, and is so absorbed by his music that he's actually quite a bore. We do start to warm to him a little when his loyal side emerges as he tries to save the hapless Giant from a beating, despite the differences that he's had with his manager.

There's one very significant aspect of *Mo' Better Blues* that recalls *School Daze* - of the two women that Bleek can't decide between, both are black but one has noticeably lighter skin than the other. If these two women were students at *School Daze*'s Mission College (Joie Lee was in *School Daze* - I'm talking about actual characters), then they would almost certainly be on opposite sides: Clarke with the upwardly mobile 'wannabes', and Indigo with the unfashionable 'jigaboos'.

Mo' Better Blues also seems to be commenting on the importance of the strong family unit in black society: Bleek is seen as only having a mother, and although for much of the film he's not much of a role model he does 'come good' in the end - not only does he marry Indigo, but they have a son together. Bleek's snapped out of his self-serving mode, and he looks forward to life with a family and without a trumpet; here's a great example of someone who has been stung into action by the 'wake up' refrain that reverberates around so much of Spike Lee's work.

It's a pity that *Mo' Better Blues* is such an unsatisfying experience, as there are reasons to believe that it could have been so much more. Denzel Washington is very good as the generally dislikeable Bleek, and Ernest Dickerson's photography brilliantly captures the hazy midnight world that these musicians inhabit. Above all else, *Mo' Better Blues* looks like a very professional piece of work - it's slick and smooth, but sadly it's also mind-numbingly dull for long stretches. And, ironically for a film where music is so central to the plot, *Mo' Better Blues* is cursed with an uncharacteristically irritating Bill Lee score.

There is one genuinely exciting moment in the film, which comes when Bleek and Giant are done over by the thugs. All of a sudden there's a huge kinetic rush, and in this well wrought sequence Spike shows just how he's able to grip an audience. The scene is filmed with a real zest and energy that, like the *Straight And Nappy* segment of *School Daze*, appears to have wandered in from a far more vital piece of work.

Spike's Stock: Mo' Better Blues marked the first time that Spike and Denzel Washington worked together. Behind the scenes, this was the last film that Spike's dad Bill provided the score for.

Trivia: She's Gotta Have It's Tracy Camilla Johns and John Canada Terrell can be glimpsed among the patrons of the Beneath the Underground club; Public Enemy frontman Flavor Flav also pops up in a brief cameo.

Verdict: A major disappointment after *Do The Right Thing*, *Mo' Better Blues* is a flabby, self-indulgent effort that did little to further Lee's career. 2/5.

Jungle Fever (1991)

Cast: Wesley Snipes (Flipper), Annabella Sciorra (Angie), Samuel L Jackson (Gator), John Turturro (Paulie), Spike Lee (Cyrus), Anthony Quinn (Lou Carbone), Ruby Dee (Lucinda), Ossie Davis (The Good Reverend Doctor Purify), Lonette McKee (Drew), Tyra Ferrell (Orin Goode), Halle Berry (Vivian), Debi Mazar (Denise), Frank Vincent (Mike), Brad Dourif (Leslie), Tim Robbins (Jerry), Theresa Randle (Inez), Michael Imperioli (James), Pamela Tyson (Angela).

Crew: Writer/Producer/Director Spike Lee, Line Producer Jon Kilik, Co-Producer Monty Ross, Editor Sam Pollard, Music Stevie Wonder & Terence Blanchard, Production Designer Wynn Thomas, Cinematography Ernest Dickerson, Costume Design Ruth E Carter.

Story: Happily married architect Flipper falls for Angie, his new secretary. This understandably outrages Flipper's wife Drew and Angie's fiancé Paulie, but it disgusts both sets of families and friends for reasons beyond infidelity: Flipper is black and Angie is white.

Flipper, who has been thrown out by Drew, is forced into staying with his mum and dad. Angie is beaten and thrown out by her father, and she and Flipper rent an apartment together. Meanwhile, Paulie declares that he's attracted to Orin Goode, a black woman; this lands him a beating from his friends. Nonetheless, a bruised and bloodied Paulie keeps the date he made with Orin.

Flipper has a brother, Gator, who's a drug addict and isn't welcome at the family home, although he sometimes comes to visit his mother when his father is out. Gator comes over and steals the family TV, and Flipper goes out into the streets to look for him. He finds his brother in a drug den, and realises the futility of trying to help him. An out of control Gator turns up at the family home, where he's shot dead by his father. Flipper and Angie separate, and although Flipper doesn't immediately move back in with Drew, it appears that a reconciliation isn't too far away.

Comment: Of the four films Spike Lee had made prior to *Jungle Fever*, only *Do The Right Thing* could be said to have been an all-round success. Crucially, *Jungle Fever* turned out to be a very impressive film, and while it didn't quite scale the heights of *Do The Right Thing* it was more than good enough to avoid its director being labelled a one-hit wonder - which could well have been the case had *Jungle Fever* flopped. In commercial terms *Jungle Fever* was Spike's biggest hit to that point, enjoying wide theatrical distribution and grossing more than $32 million at the US box office.

Jungle Fever has a lot going on in it, and is a film that's always interesting even if it doesn't always quite hit the mark. At the centre of the film is the story of Flipper and Angie, and it's the way in which their relationship affects their respective friends and families that really supplies the film with its backbone. Almost everyone in the film (except Flipper and Angie) is disgusted by the idea of an inter-racial relationship, with the exception of the kind-hearted Paulie; he seems more upset that his wife-to-be has been unfaithful, regardless of who the other man is. At face value *Jungle Fever*'s message isn't too positive, as it appears to be saying that love does actually take account of colour and that black-white relationships, such as those featured, can't possibly work. Flipper and Angie separate after hitting one bump too many in the form of belligerent peers, and Paulie is given a nasty beating from his so-called friends after he arranges a date with a black woman; the attitudes on display could hardly be described as progressive.

However, that's taking things at face value. *Jungle Fever* is almost certainly more of a comment on existing attitudes than it is a tract regarding how things should be. After all, at least Flipper, Paulie, Angie and Orin are all capable of shaking off the shackles that their respective communities have placed on them regarding who they can and can't see. Paulie and Orin's attraction seems to be the more genuine, as apart from the fact that they don't have significant others waiting at home, they seem to see each other firstly as people, with race not figuring too highly. Conversely, Flipper and Angie are well aware that even if each of them wasn't involved with someone else, what they're doing is 'wrong' - we can tell as much from the way in which they broach the matter with their supposed confidantes.

Still, if Spike Lee has shown us the ugly side of people's nature (regardless of colour - both blacks and whites are seen as intolerant), there is some hope in the film as Paulie's dogged efforts to keep his date with Orin suggest that he's going to pursue that relationship, regardless of what anyone else says or does. While this doesn't solve the problem of prejudice, it does at least signal that 'mixed' relationships aren't worth discounting; but they take more effort (and cause more rifts) than intra-racial relationships. All this feels a bit fudged - it's almost as if Spike is content to tell us how people out there think without actually getting off the fence to let us into his own way of thinking.

Besides the main plot, there's a curious backstory that runs through *Jungle Fever,* where Flipper's brother Gator plays out a cyclical existence in which he looks for money to buy drugs, gets high, then looks for more money to buy more drugs. Flipper and Gator's parents - especially their father - have largely washed their hands of this hapless drug addict, and in many ways the manner in which they disapprove of Gator's involvement with drugs is similar to where they stand on Flipper getting a white girlfriend; intolerance comes in all shapes and sizes. And although you'd hardly expect any parent to be pleased when one of their children gets hooked on drugs, you'd think that a bit of compassion and tolerance would have gone a long way towards helping Gator. As played by Samuel L Jackson, Gator is a pathetically likeable loser who behaves like little more than a performing seal - happy to do some comical jiving in the knowledge that it'll help him score a few bucks off his old mum. The scene where Flipper finds Gator in a massive crack den has to be seen to be believed - it's so squalid you'll want to take a weeklong shower.

Perhaps one of the most positive aspects of *Jungle Fever* comes with the character of Flipper. Although his infidelities do little to endear the audience to this character, he's perhaps the most successful and career-driven male character that had featured in a Lee film to that point. A successful architect, Flipper knows he's good at his job, so much so that he's painfully aware that his two white bosses are preventing him from becoming a partner - a fairly obvious example of the white man holding the black man back.

As Flipper, Wesley Snipes makes for an attractive flawed hero, and *Jungle Fever* is a film that's crammed with strong performances. Annabella Sciorra makes a decent fist of the rather bland Angie, and John Turturro is at his hangdog best as the considerate Paulie - a far cry from his spitting racist in *Do The Right Thing*. The smaller roles are filled out by a selection of fine actors, including Anthony Quinn, Ossie Davis and Ruby Dee (an item both on and off screen), and Scorsese favourite Frank Vincent. A supporting turn of particular note comes from Tyra Ferrell, who's still probably best known for playing Dr Sara Langworthy in the early episodes of TV's *ER* (1994). Her reading of Orin Goode helps supply the film with some of its quieter, more introspective moments, and it's a performance of some dignity.

Jungle Fever may be a bit of a mess when it comes to making statements about race and relationships, but it's never less than watchable. The opening credits are great fun, too, inventively featuring a set of street signs that carry the names of the cast and crew. Just don't expect the film to be the last word on mixed-race relationships.

Spike's Stock: Jungle Fever was the first Lee film to be scored by Terence Blanchard. It was also the first of five Spike films to feature Michael Imperioli in a supporting role.

Trivia: Although a Stevie Wonder song is featured in *School Daze*, *Jungle Fever* saw the realisation of one of Spike's dreams - that the singer-songwriter should actually compose tracks for a Lee film.

Verdict: Jungle Fever is a very watchable movie that may not be quite as tight as *Do The Right Thing*, but it certainly washes away the taste of *Mo' Better Blues*. Wesley does well in his one and only starring role for Spike, and Sciorra matches him every step of the way. 3/5.

4. The X Factor

After five films of undeniably variable quality, Spike started touting his biggest project to date - a biopic of Malcolm X. From the off, this was always going to be a difficult project to bring to the screen, but Warner Bros. had obviously seen enough in Spike's past work to put up $18-20 million of the budget. Spike and his producer Monty Ross knew the film would cost much more than that, and so set about pursuing several avenues (such as sales of overseas rights) for topping up the budget. In the end they had to resort to less orthodox means of getting finance to complete the film, but regardless of all the number-crunching *Malcolm X* was a massively important film for Spike, and one which really cemented his reputation as a big-hitter in the filmmaking world.

Malcolm X (1992)

Cast: Denzel Washington (Malcolm X), Angela Bassett (Betty Shabazz), Albert Hall (Baines), Delroy Lindo (West Indian Archie), Spike Lee (Shorty), Theresa Randle (Laura), Kate Vernon (Sophia), Craig Wasson (TV Host), Giancarlo Esposito (Thomas Hayer), Debi Mazar (Peg), Ernest Thomas (Sidney), Lonette McKee (Louise Little), Al Freeman Jr. (Elijah Muhammad), Christopher Plummer (Chaplain Gill), Vincent D'Onofrio (Bill Newman), Peter Boyle (Captain Green), Raye Dowell (Sister Evelyn Williams).

Crew: Director Spike Lee, Writers Arnold Perl & Spike Lee, Producers Marvin Worth & Spike Lee, Co-Producers Monty Ross & Jon Kilik, Editor Barry Alexander Brown, Music Terence Blanchard & John Coltrane, Production Designer Wynn Thomas, Cinematography Ernest Dickerson, Costume Design Ruth E Carter.

Story: During the Second World War, Malcolm Little and his friend Shorty hustle their way around Boston. Malcolm's father has been murdered by the Ku Klux Klan, and his mother institutionalised on grounds of insanity. As he gets older, Malcolm lands a job as a porter before falling in with gangster West Indian Archie. As a result of this involvement, Malcolm is sent to prison. There, a fellow inmate introduces Malcolm to the ways of Islam and the teachings of Elijah Muhammad. Malcolm dispenses with his surname, replacing it with an X.

On his release, Malcolm becomes a prominent spokesman for the Nation of Islam, and also gets married. A pilgrimage to Mecca appears to make Malcolm less militant in his views, which displeases some within the Nation. Malcolm is assassinated, presumably by dissident members of the Nation of Islam.

Comment: The opening sequence of *Malcolm X* is arguably more contentious than anything that follows in the next 3+ hours: Rodney King's terrible beating at the hands of LA policemen is intercut with shots of a burning United States flag. Although the King footage has been seen many times, it still has the power to shock; it would be a callous human being that wasn't offended by the sight of an unarmed motorist being thrashed by an armed group of men. And while the burning flag ruffled many feathers back in 1992 (rumour had it that Warner Bros. weren't going to release the movie unless the image was removed), it has taken on an added resonance following the terrorist attacks of 11 September 2001.

However, after this fiery opening, *Malcolm X* becomes a film that plays very much like any one of a number of biopics, albeit a highly polished one. The film that it perhaps has most in common with is Oliver Stone's *JFK* (1991), which was released a year earlier than *X*. Both films are epic, ambitious and controversial attempts to chronicle the lives and assassinations of important figures in American political history. And while in the early Nineties Stone may have been a more accomplished filmmaker than Lee, *Malcolm X* is nonetheless a provocative work that manages to raise many issues without deviating from the standard biopic format.

Although *Malcolm X* was a film that was widely considered to be a dangerous and inflammatory depiction of a character that many considered to be dubious, Lee's depiction of Malcolm X is fairly reverential. It's a film that shouldn't offend followers of its subject, but it also doesn't provide ammunition for Malcolm X's many detractors. It's as if Lee has consciously straddled the fence and has gone out to paint a Malcolm that is palatable to two diametrically opposed sides, which is a feat that requires no shortage of skill. It's definitely Lee's most political film, and although many may (and do) argue that Lee's interpretation of Malcolm X means that the film isn't radical enough, the fact that Spike's made a big-budget, major studio film about Malcolm X is probably a sufficient political statement in itself. By making *Malcolm X* a film short on dogma, Lee has ensured that it's a work that can't be dismissed as the work of a biased crank.

In the years since his death, Malcolm X's life and work have come to symbolise different things to different people, but to some extent his name has been conveniently reduced to a byword for black militancy - in much the same ways as Mahatma Gandhi's name is seen as being a shorthand for peace, and James Dean has come to embody disillusioned youth, and Charles Manson has become synonymous with evil. *Malcolm X* shows its central character to mean a lot more than an 'X'-emblazoned baseball cap (a Spike-designed accessory which incidentally became very popular around the time of the film's release), and concentrates on showing us Malcolm as a far more complete individual. It doesn't set him up as either hero or villain, but rather lets us into the world of a man who, like most of us, has some moments that are far better than others. It humanises Malcolm by showing us his young family, and movingly conveys how he'll both miss and be missed. Spike's Malcolm is most definitely a rounded individual that's a far cry from the angry, barking caricature portrayed by years of highly selective media footage. That said, the anger in Malcolm is most definitely on show here too, but it's just one part of the man, and not the whole.

At just over 200 minutes, *Malcolm X* is a lengthy work, but this sort of running time was needed to allow Malcolm to develop. From Malcolm's early days as a young criminal, we're taken on a journey where his initial encounter with Islam forges him into a hard-line member of the Nation, before his watershed trip to Mecca helps him revise certain aspects of his beliefs. Malcolm's a character that both black and white audiences should be able to connect with, as it's not too hard to see where he's coming from. The real strength of the film is that it always manages to remain objective and even-handed, despite its potent subject matter.

Malcolm X always manages to be engaging, but it's a film that's almost definitely more valid as education than entertainment. It's a superbly-realised project, and Denzel Washington's performance is never less than mesmerising, but the film really seems to exist to put the record straight, and to

43

let people in on what sort of man Malcolm was and how he tried to shape American attitudes in his time on earth. As such, it's a film that, like Steven Spielberg's *Schindler's List* (1993), would make for a useful addition to the history syllabuses in high schools.

The genesis of *Malcolm X*'s script makes for interesting reading: Arnold Perl wrote and directed an Oscar-nominated film, also called *Malcolm* X (1972), and Spike used Perl's writings as the starting point for his screenplay. Over the years many noted screenwriters (including David Mamet) worked on what would one day become Spike's project, but ultimately only Perl was credited as co-writer, which may allude to his active involvement in the project, when in fact Perl had died around the time that his documentary was released. Marvin Worth, who along with Perl took on associate producer duties on the 1972 *Malcolm X*, worked on the 1992 film as producer.

Although a major studio financed *Malcolm X*, Warner Bros. were reluctant to hand over any more money to Spike when he'd spent up on the project. In one of those moves that can only assist in nudging a film towards legendary status, Spike sought the financial help of a number of prominent black Americans. Thus, Bill Cosby, Janet Jackson, Michael Jordan, Tracy Chapman, Magic Johnson and quite a few others dipped into their pockets to make sure that Spike could finish the film in the way he wanted.

Spike's Stock: Most of Spike's established crew turned out for *Malcolm X*. This was the last film that Ernest Dickerson photographed for Lee, as the outstanding cinematographer was keen to move over into directing - around the same time as *X*, Dickerson directed *Juice* (1992).

Malcolm X saw both Ossie Davis and Giancarlo Esposito appear for the fourth time in a Lee movie. Although there's no John Turturro this time, his brother Nick keeps the family name in there.

Trivia: Albert Hall - the judge from TV's *Ally McBeal* (1997) - plays an inmate who introduces Malcolm to the teachings of Elijah Muhammad. In Michael Mann's *Ali* (2001), Elijah Muhammad is played by none other than Albert Hall.

The long Hall? Rent *Malcolm X* and another Albert Hall movie - Francis Ford Coppola's *Apocalypse Now Redux* (1979/2001)- and you'll have to spend nearly 7 hours to get through that particular double bill.

In real life, Ossie Davis read the eulogy at Malcolm X's funeral.

Despite much hype, *Malcolm X* left the Oscars empty handed; Denzel Washington was beaten to the best actor gong by Al Pacino, while Ruth Carter's costume design lost out to that in *Bram Stoker's Dracula* (1992).

Verdict: In many ways *Malcolm X* is one of those films that you admire without totally warming to. It's hard to pick fault with the production, and it's almost impossible to not be impressed by the sheer scale of the project. Everything about it is rock-solid, but only Denzel's performance is spectacular. 4/5.

5. The Double Truth, Ruth

As expected, *Malcolm X* ruffled plenty of feathers across the US, but proved disappointing at the box office, where its domestic takings stalled at around the $48 million mark. Not that that's an amount to be sniffed at - it was, and remains, Spike's biggest hit to date - but after all the blood, sweat and tears that went into the making of the movie (not to mention all the hype), it wouldn't have been unreasonable to have expected the film to gross at least $25 million more.

Malcolm X also appeared to mark a period where audiences got a little disenchanted with the high profile of its director; Spike Lee was understandably doing all he could to plug his film, and although it got its share of the audience it seems that many people made it their last appointment with Spike. His follow-up films all fared poorly at the box office, with the four titles that followed *Malcolm X* pulling in a meagre $36 million between them. At this point it seems that Spike Lee was in danger of becoming another Woody Allen - a New York director whose name always guarantees a bit of buzz whenever a film's imminent, yet rarely does anything of note at the box office. (Incidentally, Woody's biggest box office hit, *Hannah And Her Sisters* (1986), took $40 million - a figure not too far off Spike's number one grosser).

The poor response to the films Spike made from 1994 to 1996 was not entirely unwarranted; only two of the four should have done better, while the other two were fortunate to make anything like the money that they did.

Crooklyn (1994)

Cast: Alfre Woodard (Carolyn), Delroy Lindo (Woody), Isaiah Washington (Vic), David Patrick Kelly (Tony Eyes), Zelda Harris (Troy), Carlton Williams (Clinton), Sharif Rashed (Wendell), Tse-Mach Washington (Joseph), Christopher Knowings (Nate), Jose Zuniga (Tommy La La), Spike Lee (Snuffy), Vondie Curtis-Hall (Uncle Brown), Bokeem Woodbine (Richard), Joie Lee (Aunt Maxine), Frances Foster (Aunt Song).

Crew: Producer/Director Spike Lee, Writers Cinqué Lee & Joie Lee & Spike Lee, Associate Producers Cinqué Lee & Joie Lee, Co-Producer Monty Ross, Executive Producer Jon Kilik, Editor Barry Alexander Brown, Music Terence Blanchard, Production Designer Wynn Thomas, Cinematography Arthur Jafa, Costume Design Ruth E Carter.

Story: Brooklyn, the early 1970s. Musician Woody Carmichael and his schoolteacher wife Carolyn have five children - Clinton, Wendell, Nate, Joseph and Troy. During the summer holidays, Carolyn decides that it would be good if Troy - the only girl - was to spend a while with her Aunt Song in the south. Troy isn't too pleased when her Aunt tries to interfere with her clothes and hair, and the opening stretch of her holiday isn't too pleasurable. As time progresses, Troy bonds with her cousin Viola, and the two girls manage to teach each other some new things. Following an unpleasant incident over dinner, Troy signals that she'd like to go home. Back in Brooklyn, a cancer-stricken Carolyn dies.

Comment: After the gargantuan effort required to make *Malcolm X*, Spike scaled things down considerably with *Crooklyn*. Low-key in every sense, *Crooklyn* appeared to be made as much for therapeutic reasons as anything else; that a film emerged at the end of it probably seemed like a bonus for Spike, as it seems to be an exercise more concerned with process than results.

You can almost sense Spike getting his breath back as he directs this gentle, modest tale. Although it can be - and has been - lazily labelled as his most personal work, this almost certainly isn't the case; it's definitely his most autobiographical film, but that doesn't automatically make it highly personal (*He Got Game* seems to be much closer to Spike's heart). If anything, it feels as if *Crooklyn* was probably more of a product of Spike's siblings Cinqué and Joie, who shared writing and producing duties with their more famous brother. You get the impression that the enthusiasm of his brother and sister might have helped nudge the (understandably) drained Spike along with his directing of *Crooklyn*, and even though the end result is professional enough it seems well within the capabilities of the man behind *Do The Right Thing*, *Jungle Fever* and *Malcolm X*.

Like Gary Oldman's largely autobiographical *Nil By Mouth* (1997), *Crooklyn* uses the device of seeing the world through the eyes of a young girl. Although the girl in *Crooklyn* is more of a central (and composite) character than the one in *Nil By Mouth*, and Lee's film is far less extreme in terms of content, there are distinct similarities in the ways in which both directors have recalled their early urban existences. There's some affection in there, but little sentimentality.

The importance of the family unit is a theme at the forefront of *Crooklyn*, and recalls *Mo' Better Blues* in the way in which a stable home life is presented as being the key to a happy and fulfilled existence. Despite the hardships that life sometimes throws their way, the Carmichaels are a good bunch of people, and the Lee siblings have gone as far as giving Carolyn and Woody the same jobs (teacher and musician, respectively) as Spike, Joie and Cinqué's parents. Carolyn's tragic death at the film's close leaves no doubt as to the vital role she played in binding the family together, and with her gone we're well aware that it's a blow that the Carmichaels will find hard to recover from.

Crooklyn carries echoes of *School Daze* in the way in which Troy's Aunt Song is a black person who is trying to get to a place where she'll feel superior to others of her race. With the way in which she tries to remodel Troy, Song is clearly a more mature model of the 'wannabe'. The parallels are reinforced through Song's attempted straightening of Troy's hair - *Straight and Nappy*, anyone?

Curiously, and despite the film's title, *Crooklyn* paints a picture of early '70s Brooklyn that's largely free of crime and trouble, and is surely a reimagining of both time and place. Lee always claimed that he intended *Crooklyn* to be essentially a family film - and in terms of audience, subject and crew it most definitely is - but there's an odd lack of authenticity in seeing a Brooklyn that's mostly free of tension, violence and swearing. Maybe that's partly because of the way in which Lee's depicted the borough in the past, and watching this idealised version of those streets will be a different kind of shock for those who've been primed on a diet of the likes of *Do The Right Thing*.

There's not much to get excited about in *Crooklyn* - it's well acted, with three-time Emmy winner Alfre Woodard bringing a lot to the role of Carolyn and young Zelda Harris making a good job of the pivotal part of Troy. Other than that, *Crooklyn* quickly becomes a bore and plays a bit like a home movie; fine if you're a member of the Lee family, but if you're not it's about as much fun as spending an evening with someone else's holiday snaps.

Spike's Stock: The usual suspects, bar cinematographer Arthur Jafa. Spike appeared to be between DoPs when he made *Crooklyn*, and this was to be the only film that Jafa would shoot for the director.

Trivia: Zelda Harris landed the role of Troy after attending an open audition - the then-nine year-old beat over 1000 other children to the part.

Verdict: Spike's to be applauded for making something that's a little more family-oriented than his usual fare, but *Crooklyn* (a fairly misleading title) is a lumpen, rambling work that sorely outstays its welcome. 2/5.

Clockers (1995)

Cast: Harvey Keitel (Rocco Klein), John Turturro (Larry Mazilli), Keith David (Andre the Giant), Delroy Lindo (Rodney Little), Mekhi Phifer (Strike), Isaiah Washington (Victor), Steve White (Darryl Adams), Michael Imperioli (Detective Jo-Jo), Regina Taylor (Iris Jeeter), Pee Wee Love (Tyrone Jeeter), Sticky Fingaz (Scientific), Mike Starr (Thumper), Paul Calderon (Jesus), Michael Badalucco (Cop 1).

Crew: Director Spike Lee, Writers Richard Price & Spike Lee, Producers Martin Scorsese & Jon Kilik & Spike Lee, Co-Producer Richard Price, Executive Producer Monty Ross, Editor Sam Pollard, Music Terence Blanchard & Bruce Hornsby, Production Designer Andrew McAlpine, Cinematography Malik Hassan Sayeed, Costume Design Ruth E Carter.

Story: In one of Brooklyn's housing projects, round-the-clock drug dealers (known as 'clockers') work the streets. Young dealer Strike is keen to move onto bigger things in the drug trade, and makes this known to supplier Rodney. Rodney sets Strike a task - the killing of a belligerent fast-food restaurant manager - that is intended to demonstrate Strike's loyalty.

On his way to carrying out the task, Strike bumps into his brother Victor. Victor is an honest, hard-working sort, but after a few drinks he tells Strike that he knows someone who can take care of the manager. After the two brothers separate, Strike is seen heading for the restaurant, where he has a conversation with the manager.

The restaurant manager is found murdered, and NYPD detectives Rocco Klein and Larry Mazilli move in to investigate the case. Victor confesses to the crime and is taken into custody, but Klein disregards Victor's story, choosing to pursue Strike. Strike comes under a lot of pressure from both Klein and Rodney, with the latter worried that Strike may implicate him. Klein - who's well aware of Rodney's criminal activities - gets Rodney arrested, but even from the lock-up Rodney is able to arrange for someone to try and kill Strike. The would-be killer is shot by a young boy that Strike has befriended, but Klein sees that the boy doesn't get into too much trouble. Pursued by Rodney, Strike heads for the police station and is interrogated by Klein. Klein has lost all patience with Strike, and starts pushing him around the room. The interrogation is interrupted by Strike's mother, who reveals that it was Victor who killed the fast-food manager. Klein drives Strike to Penn Station and tells him never to return to the area. Strike boards a train, and is seen heading away from the city and towards a new start.

Comment: Clockers is one of Lee's most effective films, and vividly conveys the hopelessness of the dead-end existence of the street dealers and their associates. Having shifted the main emphasis of Richard Price's novel from policeman Rocco Klein to young pusher Strike, Lee has pulled off the tricky task of making the dealer something more than a one-dimensional lowlife. While Strike is painted as human, he clearly isn't intended to be a hero - his criminal activities do little to elicit audience sympathy. The situation is the same for his apparent willingness to let his brother take the rap for a murder. However, with an interest in trains and a good-natured side, Strike is presented as being a kid whose criminal leanings are a symptom of his environment; in other words, he's a victim of circumstance.

The police are portrayed in a mostly favourable light, with white detectives Klein and Mazilli shown as being guys with a tough job to do, as is black local officer Andre. Klein and Andre have a real desire to see the criminals taken off the streets, and both are desperate to stop the kids in the project from entering the criminal world. Despite Klein's frequent strong-arm tactics, the police are shown to be fundamentally decent; even when Andre gives Strike a real beating it's clear that such action stems from the frustration at seeing a young boy facing ruin.

Although *Clockers* tells a very grim tale, Lee doesn't allow the film to end on a sour note, as Strike is seen heading off for (presumably) better things, and it's made clear that it's possible to escape a life of crime. The salvation-imbued ending bears an uncanny resemblance to that of Abel Ferrara's *Bad Lieutenant* (1992) - in both films, Harvey Keitel plays a New York policeman who drops a young criminal (or more than one) at a transport depot, with the orders to leave town for good.

As one of the strongest movies in the Lee filmography, it's interesting to note how *Clockers* wasn't a project that was initiated by the director. The film was originally to be directed by Martin Scorsese with Robert De Niro as the star, but the two opted to make *Casino* (1995) instead. Scorsese's involvement in *Clockers* was reduced to co-producing the film, and another

Scorsese favourite - Harvey Keitel - stepped into the lead role. Bronx writer Richard Price (*The Wanderers* (1979), *Sea Of Love* (1989)) had worked with Scorsese on other projects including *The Color Of Money* (1986), *New York Stories* (1989) and *Mad Dog And Glory* (1992), and although the change in director must have surprised the scribe it didn't stop him and Lee from producing a tight screenplay.

Despite all the hard work, the wide distribution of the film (on a scale similar to *Malcolm X*) and the presence of Harvey Keitel (a resurgent star in the mid-1990s), *Clockers* performed poorly at the box office with a domestic gross of just over $13 million - the same as *Crooklyn*.

Spike's Stock: John Turturro popped up again, taking second billing for his largely silent role. British-born actor Delroy Lindo notched up his third appearance in a Lee film, while Spike himself appeared in a low-key part.

On the production side, *Clockers* was the first Lee film where Wynn Thomas didn't take on production designing duties; his role was filled by Andrew McAlpine, who'd won a BAFTA for his work on Jane Campion's *The Piano* (1993). *Clockers* was the last film to feature the involvement of Lee's longtime producer and old college buddy Monty Ross, whose contributions to Lee's feature films stretched all the way back to *She's Gotta Have It*.

Trivia: Clockers is the second successive Spike Lee film where Isaiah Washington plays a character named Vic.

Michael Badalucco has a small role as a cop, and in a few years he'd move to the other side of the law as the notorious serial killer in *Summer Of Sam*.

Richard Price's source novel was actually set in New Jersey, but for the film the action was moved through the Holland Tunnel to New York. Perhaps not too surprising, given that it's both Scorsese and Lee's home city, and one which they've used as a backdrop for their films on numerous occasions.

Verdict: The joke's on Scorsese, as *Clockers* is a much better film than *Casino*. Don't get me wrong - *Casino*'s pretty good, but is ultimately little more than a reheated *Goodfellas* (1990). *Clockers*, on the other hand, is a searing portrait of a nightmare world which boasts another powerhouse performance from Harvey Keitel, as well as outstanding turns from Mekhi Phifer and Isaiah Washington as the two brothers. With much of the dialogue presented in an undiluted street vernacular, *Clockers* is perhaps a bit too inaccessible for some tastes, but is well worth persevering with. 5/5.

Girl 6 (1996)

Cast: Theresa Randle (Girl 6), Isaiah Washington (Shoplifter), Debi Mazar (Girl 39), Gretchen Mol (Girl 12), Madonna (Boss 3), Spike Lee (Jimmy), Michael Imperioli (Caller 30), John Turturro (Murray the Agent), Quentin Tarantino (QT), Ron Silver (Director 2), Peter Berg (Caller 1).

Crew: Producer/Director Spike Lee, Writer Suzan-Lori Parks, Executive Producer Jon Kilik, Editor Sam Pollard, Music Prince & Georges Bizet, Production Designer Ina Mayhew, Cinematography Malik Hassan Sayeed, Costume Design Sandra Hernandez.

Story: After a humiliating experience at an audition, an aspiring New York actress is dropped by her agent. Struggling for money, she then finds that her acting teacher no longer wants to work with her. Unable to make enough money to survive on, she tries for a job as a phone-sex operator. She gets the job, and is assigned the title Girl 6. She acquits herself well, and justifies the work to herself on the grounds that it utilises her acting skills.

Outside of work, Girl 6 has little going on; she spends some time with her baseball-loving next-door neighbour, and is pursued by her ex-husband. With so little of meaning in her personal life, she throws herself into her work. With the help of her next-door neighbour, she gets things in perspective and realises that the phone-sex work isn't really going to be her long-term career. With a new sense of purpose, she heads for Los Angeles with the intention of picking up her acting career.

Comment: Ten years on from his debut *She's Gotta Have It*, Spike Lee returned to similar territory with *Girl 6*. Unfortunately, what could - and should - have been an interesting and enjoyable picture actually turned out to be about as unsatisfying as Lee's first film, and was perhaps even more disappointing on the grounds that this was the work of an experienced director.

Girl 6 and *She's Gotta Have It* are the only two Lee features in which a woman takes centre stage. Sure, there have been earlier and later films that have had major roles for females - *Jungle Fever*, *Crooklyn* and *Summer Of Sam* spring immediately to mind - but none of these films have focused exclusively on the female characters.

Spike himself has said that he wouldn't be too bothered if people saw *Girl 6* as a companion piece to his debut, and it's not hard to see why people might reasonably reach such a conclusion. Apart from the aforementioned central female characters, the two films share several themes - self-discovery, self-empowerment, sex. Perhaps more pertinently, both films aren't concerned with racial themes; both Nola Darling and Girl 6 are black, but their skin colour isn't an issue.

The most obvious way in which people will connect *Girl 6* with *She's Gotta Have It* is through *Girl 6*'s opening sequence, where our eponymous protagonist uses one of Nola Darling's monologues as an audition piece. Lee fans will instantly recognise the piece, and those used to hearing it spoken by Tracy Camilla Johns can marvel at the novelty of hearing it being read by Theresa Randle. Still perhaps best known for playing the female lead in the live-action adaptation of Todd McFarlane's *Spawn* (1997), Randle is an interesting performer and it's a pity that *Girl 6* did so little to further her career.

Perhaps Spike Lee wanted to make *Girl 6* as a compensatory measure for having made a slew of male-dominated pictures since Nola Darling's screen outing back in 1986, but if this is the case it perhaps proves that he should stick to what he knows best. While Girl 6 is a likeable enough character - far more likeable than Nola, as it happens - the role is still painfully underdeveloped and underwritten, and by the end of the film the audience has learned little about her. All we can say about her is that she's an actress who temporarily ditches that profession for a phone-sex job. Just like *She's Gotta Have It*, the film doesn't really seem to be about anything very much, which is all the more surprising seeing as the film was written by a female playwright, Suzan-Lori Parks. Other than the familiar milieu of New York, Lee seems totally at odds with his subject matter, and in the end *Girl 6* plays out as a hollow, superficial effort that's technically superior to *She's Gotta Have It* but is otherwise no improvement.

Of course not every film needs to have a message, and to say that *Girl 6* is a bad film because it's not really about anything would be unfair. However, if you don't have a valid point to make then your film should entertaining, and on this score *Girl 6* is also found wanting. *Girl 6* is probably the biggest misfire of Lee's career to date. It isn't funny, sexy or interesting, and the parade of flashy cameos only serves to irritate. As already mentioned, Theresa Randle's a good actress, but that's not enough when the material is this weak.

Girl 6 cost $12 million to make, but despite a wide release, it made less than $5 million in the domestic market. This made it the poorest earner out of all of Spike's films to that point - not much of a way to mark a decade in the feature film business.

Spike's Stock: This was the third outing in a Spike film for both Theresa Randle and Debi Mazar. Both actresses had previously featured in *Jungle Fever* and *Malcolm X*. Designers Ina Mayhew (production) and Sandra Hernandez (costume) both worked with Lee for the first time here.

Trivia: Quentin Tarantino makes a mercifully brief appearance as film director QT. In times to come, things between Spike and Quentin would become pretty strained, with Lee objecting to the gratuitous racial slurs peppered throughout *Jackie Brown* (1997).

Verdict: Girl 6. Film 2/5.

Get On The Bus (1996)

Cast: Isaiah Washington (Kyle), Albert Hall (Craig), Charles S Dutton (George), Andre Braugher (Flip), Ossie Davis (Jeremiah), Steve White (Mike), Frank Clem (Jefferson), Richard Belzer (Rick), Joie Lee (Jindal), Bernie Mac (Jay).

Crew: Executive Producer/Director Spike Lee, Writer Reggie Rock Bythewood, Producers Bill Borden & Reuben Cannon & Barry Rosenbush, Editor Leander T Sales, Music Terence Blanchard & Kenneth 'Babyface' Edmonds, Production Designer Ina Mayhew, Cinematography Elliot Davis, Costume Design Sandra Hernandez.

Story: 1995. Three days before Louis Farrakhan's Million Man March in Washington, a busload of men set off on the 2000-mile journey from Los Angeles. The travelling party is all black, but are from a variety of different backgrounds; there's a policeman, an actor, a film student, a gay couple, a reformed gangster, plus several others. Along the way, the group find that they are separated by their many differences, and things get even more strained when the bus breaks down and the replacement vehicle is manned by a white Jewish driver. After some heated discussions, the driver decides that it would be wrong for him to drive the bus into Washington, and leaves the bus at one of the rest stops; George, the party organiser, takes over.

As the journey nears its conclusion, the eldest member of the party suffers a heart attack, and later dies in hospital. Because of this, the group misses the main events at the march (such as the speeches), but nonetheless finds that it is united by their similarities, and the negative feelings of earlier on are banished.

Comment: Spike followed up the heavyweight *Clockers* and the lamentable *Girl 6* with this atypically light and warm drama, which sees twenty men cooped up on a bus together for a period of three days. With such a long time to be forced into one another's company, things soon veer towards the tetchy, and Lee treats us to the sort of up-close character study previously on show in the likes of *Do The Right Thing* and *Jungle Fever*. And in terms of characterisation, *Get On The Bus* is pretty much Lee's most successful film; there's little in the way of plot, so Spike is able to focus his energies on examining the relationships between the men that are holed up on the bus.

These people are effectively captive (as is the camera), and Spike's able to get under the skin of these characters without multiple backstories getting in the way. It's a simplistic premise, but one that brings rewarding results.

Thematically, *Get On The Bus* is a riff on the ideas presented in *School Daze*, and looks at the bickering that exists between members of the black community. Although his canvas here is narrower than it was in his second film (a bus is a good deal smaller than a college campus), there's a rich assortment of characters that represent more than simply 'jigaboos' or 'wannabes'.

Unlike *School Daze*, however, *Get On The Bus* has a generally more positive outcome. While *School Daze* ends with its main character shouting for everyone to wake up (and we're not sure if they actually do or not), here they've all woken up before the movie ends. Although it could be argued that it takes the death of the elderly Jeremiah to pull everyone together, *Get On The Bus* nonetheless stands as an example of how dialogue can help people to reach an understanding - regardless of other differences. By the end of *Get On The Bus*, the men are saddened to have missed the bulk of the Million Man March, but what they've learned is infinitely more vital than they would have if they had bickered all the way to Washington, attended the march, and then boarded the bus back to LA. Lee's forced his characters to meet each other half way, and they realise that being black is something that they can all share in and look to as a common bond.

Besides the message(s) that Spike Lee manages to convey within the confines of a meagre bus, there's a feeling that *Get On The Bus'* primary reason for existence was to chronicle the Million Man March. This was an important event, and by shooting the film on location and including actual footage of the march itself, Spike Lee did his part in helping to document the event.

On the whole, *Get On The Bus* is a real success, and the brilliant ensemble acting (which received a special award at the Berlin International Film Festival) makes for extremely pleasurable viewing. First-time Lee cinematographer Elliot Davis has photographed the film in an unfussy, unobtrusive manner that lends an authentic documentary feel (although the occasional changes in film stock may irk some viewers), and this goes a long way towards making the viewer focus on these characters.

Get On The Bus was financed in a rather unique way - in keeping with the spirit of the way in which *Malcolm X* was latterly funded, the film received financial contributions from 15 prominent black Americans, including Lee himself, writer Reggie Rock Bythewood, and actors Will Smith, Danny Glover and Wesley Snipes. Between them, the collective raised the entire budget (around $2.5 million), and the film bore the credit 'A 15 Black Men Production'. This method of funding makes a lot of sense, as it would be ironic if the message of both the film and Louis Farrakhan's march were to be ignored; with these themes in mind, it seems only right that a group of black men should unite to get such a project off the ground.

Spike's Stock: Relative newcomer to the fold Albert Hall features in his second film for Lee, following his major turn in *Malcolm X*. Other returning actors include Isaiah Washington and Ossie Davis.

As far as the crew went, Terence Blanchard was one of the few longtime Lee associates to have worked on the film. Ina Mayhew and Sandra Hernandez had both worked on *Girl 6*, but *Get On The Bus* saw new faces responsible for producing, editing and photographing the movie.

Trivia: Four Spikes and you're out? Isaiah Washington's appearance in *Get On The Bus* made it the fourth consecutive Lee film he'd appeared in; it was also his last to date. The same pattern holds true for another prominent actor, Samuel L Jackson, who appeared in four in a row for Spike (*School Daze* through *Jungle Fever*) before apparently falling off the director's radar.

Get On The Bus was released on the first anniversary of the Million Man March.

Look out for *National Lampoon* favourite Randy Quaid in an uncredited role as a state trooper.

Verdict: After *Girl 6*, you'd have been forgiven for dreading the next Spike Lee film. Thankfully, *Get On The Bus* was a big improvement over its predecessor, and chronicled a massive event with charm, wit and genuine warmth. Probably the most underrated of Spike's films to date, and well worth seeking out. 4/5.

6. Here's To You, Jackie Robinson

Spike's one of those directors who has a fairly high-profile persona away from the movie set. Known for contributing his frequently controversial opinions to many a hot topic, he's also become one of the most prominent celebrity sports fans. In the US there are a number of actors and directors who make no secret of their love for particular sports and/or teams, and those who immediately spring to mind include Jack Nicholson, Woody Allen and Matthew Modine. However, Spike is arguably the #1 celebrity fan, not just because of his vocal support but because he passionately follows two teams across two different sports.

Basketball is his favourite game, with baseball coming in a close second. Many people simply align him with basketball, maybe because he's often pictured in his courtside seat at Madison Square Garden. As an avid fan of the New York Knickerbockers (widely known as the 'Knicks') his animated sideline gesturing makes for good value for the sports pages and the live cameras that relay the Knicks games - indeed, Spike's reactions to key moments have become a staple of Knicks home games that no self-respecting TV director misses. Jack Nicholson may be the more famous than Spike, but his obsessive support of the Los Angeles Lakers - while well documented in the media - somehow fails to capture the imagination in the same way as Lee's intense endorsement of the Knicks.

Keeping it local, and Spike's baseball team of choice is the world-famous New York Yankees. A huge fan of the team, it nonetheless appears that Spike views baseball in more general terms than he does basketball. While he would always want the Yankees to walk away with the World Series, there's the distinct impression that he's more a fan of the overall game than anything else. On the other hand, the Knicks are the be-all and end-all to Spike as far as the NBA is concerned.

As anyone remotely familiar with Spike's films will have noticed, sport plays an important role in his work. Basketball and baseball seem to be a part of his life to the extent that there's a distinct overlap between the role sport plays in his life and work, and what he draws from it in real life is often ploughed back into his films.

As early on in his career as *She's Gotta Have It*, Lee incorporated the lively sports debate into his work. Anyone who's seen (or read) Spike talking about sport will be well aware that, as with most subjects, he doesn't hold back. In *She's Gotta Have It*, Boston Celtics legend Larry Bird is up for debate: Jamie Overstreet argues that 'the white boy' is the best player in the NBA, while Spike's Mars Blackmon (who else?) is having none of this. Mars tries to avoid admitting Bird's quality by calling him the 'ugliest motherfucker in the NBA,' but even in this we can sense that Mars is well aware of how good Larry Bird actually is. With this amusing scene, Lee has perfectly captured the sort of banter that occurs between sports fans the world over, and because he's always been such a big fan we know that this comes from the heart as opposed to being some glib observation.

Although most of the films that followed *She's Gotta Have It* didn't have baseball or basketball at the forefront, sport nonetheless plays a supporting role in many of Lee's films: *Do The Right Thing*'s Mookie (Lee again) is seldom seen out of his #42 Jackie Robinson shirt (more of Robinson later), and in the scene in which he discusses baseball with Vito local white man Clifton walks past in a Larry Bird/Boston Celtics shirt; *Crooklyn* takes place around the time of the Knicks' 1973 title triumph; and the set of *Clockers* saw a famous discussion between Lee and Isaiah Washington, with the actor point blank refusing to be filmed carrying a Knicks bag on account of his steadfast allegiance to the Houston Rockets.

Of course, *He Got Game* is the Lee film where sport really came out of the shadows, and with that film it's as if Spike could completely let rip and wax lyrical about one of the loves of his life. And although it can't be labelled either a film that's solely about basketball or just another sports movie, basketball certainly features heavily throughout the course. *He Got Game* presented Lee with an extended opportunity to work with an NBA player - Milwaukee Bucks guard Ray Allen, who took on the major role of Jesus Shuttlesworth. Spike quite logically explains that it was easier to teach a basketball player to act than it would have been to coach an actor to play basketball, but this aside Spike must have been thrilled to have been working with an NBA star in such a big way - let's not forget that Lee's a fan, and there must have been some pretty long and lively on-set conversations between the director and his young star. Just to make things even better for

Spike - as if making a basketball-themed film with Ray Allen wasn't enough - major NBA players Shaquille O'Neal, Scottie Pippen, Reggie Miller and Michael Jordan all contributed brief cameos to the film. Jordan, of course, knew Spike from way back through the Nike TV ads they collaborated on, while Lee and Miller have a bit of history together - the Indiana Pacers star had a very public spat with the ardent Knicks fan.

Changing sports and moving ahead to one of Spike's most recent features, and *Summer Of Sam* was a film chock-full of baseball references. As David Berkowitz's killing spree occurred in the summer of 1977, you can't help but feel that a lot of the appeal to Spike in making a film set then lay in that time coinciding with the Yankees' incredible World Series win of that year. As journo Jimmy Breslin informs us at the close of *Sam*, the 1977 series was won by the Yankees largely because of Reggie Jackson's three home runs in the sixth game. In a time that saw, among other things, the Son of Sam walking the streets, the death of Elvis Presley, and the blackout and looting in New York, it's clear that Spike considers the achievements of Jackson and his Yankee team-mates to be as notable an event as anything else that was going on.

The most sport-themed Spike Lee movie is one that is yet to make it into production - his telling of the Jackie Robinson story. Robinson is a legendary figure in baseball, as apart from his on-field exploits with the Brooklyn (now LA) Dodgers he went down in history as the player that broke the colour barrier. In 1947, Robinson became the first African-American to play in the Major League, and he did a magnificent job of working for racial equality; not only was Jackie one of the best players ever to take to the field, but his tireless work to unite people across all races and cultures made him a hero to blacks and whites across America. His story is a fascinating one, and Lee has a script ready, but sadly funding for the project hasn't been forthcoming. Although Robinson was much more than a baseball player, such a project would understandably be viewed as a baseball picture, and that sub-genre doesn't have a great record at the box office. And out of line with most of Lee's other work, it would be a hard film to sell overseas, given that baseball is so US-centric (it may be called the World Series, but it's not a global event). So, we're still waiting on Spike's Jackie Robinson film appearing, although if and when it does it's almost certainly to feature more baseball than *He Got Game* has basketball sequences. Meanwhile, baseball obsessives will have to make do with the Reggie Jackson material that peppers *Summer Of Sam*.

Although it's not a Lee feature film and it wasn't made under anything like typical circumstances, Spike directed a short sports film that was played at the post-11 September 2001 Concert For New York. This short, which ran about three and a half minutes, featured footage of the Yankees and their famous stadium. Spike's fellow New Yorker (and *Clockers* collaborator) Martin Scorsese weighed in with his own short effort, as did Woody Allen. And on the musical side of things The Who performed *Baba O' Riley* - a song that features prominently in *Summer Of Sam*, which in turn features liberal footage of the Yankees.

As someone who's often essayed the differences that exist between races and cultures, sport - particularly basketball - seems to represent to Lee an aspect of life that, like the aforementioned Jackie Robinson, rises above racial barriers. Spike Lee enjoys basketball, and it's clear that he sees it as something to be played and enjoyed by all; Mars' reservations in *She's Gotta Have It* are not necessarily the views of the director. Sport rises above racial politics, and in many ways his love of basketball (and baseball) must act as a valuable outlet where Spike is able to enjoy something that's free of the contentious streak that runs through the bulk of his work - even politically motivated filmmakers need some time off.

7. Epiphany

As good as *Get On The Bus* was, it did absolutely nothing to arrest Lee's decline in box office terms. Although he was still most definitely a name director, the hard fact remained that only two of Spike's films - *Jungle Fever* and *Malcolm X* - had made more than $30 million in the domestic market. Since *Malcolm X* there hadn't been so much as a whiff of a hit, and all subsequent films had been damned by faint praise - so it's not as even if Spike could find solace in good critical notices.

As his feature films were enduring scant exposure and poor responses, Spike arrived at what was a crucial time in his career. Just like when he'd directed *Do The Right Thing* a good eight years earlier, there was a feeling that Spike had better produce something special out of the hat. Having experienced little success in theatrical features for some time, he altered his game plan somewhat and shifted across formats, into the realm of the documentary.

4 Little Girls (1997)

With: Chris McNair, Maxine McNair, Helen Pegues, Queen Nunn, Arthur Hanes Jr., Bill Baxley, Ossie Davis, Reggie White, Bill Cosby, Spike Lee, Shirley Wesley King, Jesse Jackson.

Crew: Director Spike Lee, Producers Spike Lee & Sam Pollard, Executive Producer Sheila Nevins, Associate Producer Michele Forman, Editor Sam Pollard, Music Terence Blanchard, Sound JT Tagaki, Cinematography Ellen Kuras.

Story: A documentary concerning the bombing of a Birmingham, Alabama church on 15 September 1963. The attack, which was on the Sixteenth Street Baptist Church, killed four girls - Addie May Collins, Denise McNair, Carol Robertson, and Cynthia Wesley.

Comment: It's easy to view *4 Little Girls* as simply a film that conveys the tragedy of events that occurred nearly 35 years earlier, but it's so much more than that. In many ways the civil rights struggle from that time isn't that well documented; although we're aware of the gist of what went on, there aren't enough books or films that go into detail about specific incidents. *4 Little Girls* acts as both a painful reminder of the injustice that was prevalent at the time and an alert to current situations - when the film appeared, the bombing of black churches in the south was again figuring in the news.

If *Malcolm X* is a film that would act as a useful educational tool, then *4 Little Girls* is even more suited to the classroom. Unlike *X*, *4 Little Girls* is a bona fide documentary as opposed to a re-enactment, and it's a draining, sobering experience. Fleeting shots of the four dead girls being laid out in the mortuary really are the stuff of nightmares, and it's to the credit of both Spike Lee and Sam Pollard that these images are used in a highly sensitive way. The shots don't linger so as to be at all distasteful or exploitative, but are up on screen for just long enough so as to allow the real horror of this tale to hit home. As words on a page, the killing of four girls (the eldest of whom was aged fourteen years) makes for repugnant reading, but it's only when you see the images of their bodies and hear their families talk about them that you realise just what this all meant - or rather means.

The girls in the film are not made out to be martyrs - after all, they had no choice regarding what was to happen to them - but their deaths are held up as symbols representative of the sort of 'results' that are achieved through extreme racism. This is where Lee and Pollard have managed to pull off a really tricky aspect of the film, as they've managed to make *4 Little Girls* a film that tells the story of these girls and their families as well as highlighting important aspects of the civil rights struggle. Many filmmakers would have settled on painting either the bigger or the smaller picture, but in *4 Little Girls* we get to see both the way in which this event affected the people directly involved as well as the impact that was made on the whole country.

The message in the film is perhaps pretty obvious, and in some ways telling people how a group of kids was murdered by mindless racists is all that it needed. However, there is a real spirit of hope in evidence here, and the bombing and the killings are shown to have added more grit and determination to the civil rights struggle. There's an immense dignity that exudes from the bereaved families, too: Chris McNair (Denise's father) and the other family members that are interviewed never come across as bitter or hateful. Like the bombing itself, this attitude can only serve to make the anti-racist element stronger. At the other end of the spectrum, there's then-governor and rabid segregationist George Wallace, and he's a pretty hard act to take on any level, but especially when compared to the demeanour of the aggrieved families. Although we see Wallace as a frail old person, we're left in little doubt as to what Spike wants us to think of the man through the inclusion of footage relaying how Wallace opposed intended racial integration at the University of Alabama.

From a technical point of view, *4 Little Girls* was a film that saw Spike Lee progress as a filmmaker. Making a feature-length documentary added a lot to his filmmaking vocabulary, and through his skilful interweaving of new interviews with archive footage we can see how he's become acquainted with the more rigid bounds of the documentary format. As we all know, documentary film can be selective in what it shows the viewer, but regardless of that Lee is working with as-is material here. That he manages to assemble a work that's not only informative, but is as gripping as anything else he's ever made shows how the format made him into a more thoughtful, economical and astute director.

It would be wrong, however, to give Spike all the credit for the film's success. Sam Pollard has obviously brought a wealth of experience to the project, as he was a documentary filmmaker for some 25 years before gaining more prominence as Spike's editor. Out of all of Spike's films, *4 Little Girls* owes the most to its editor - scenes like the aforementioned mortuary one could easily have been bungled in the hands of a less skilled splicer.

Although *4 Little Girls* is a compelling and upsetting work, it's not without its flaws. The intrusive appearances of celebrities - most notably Bill Cosby - are in danger of making this delicately-poised film fall off of its tightrope, and such moments veer towards reducing the situation to some sort of cause célèbre. Still, *4 Little Girls* has much to recommend it, and as well as standing as a terrific documentary in its own right, it is to be valued as a film that saw Spike Lee take a massive step towards maturity as a filmmaker.

Made for HBO, the film enjoyed a very limited theatrical run which acted as a platform for both the film's TV showing and the bid for Oscar success.

Spike's Stock: Quite a few of Spike's established crew worked on this, with editor Sam Pollard also wearing a producer's hat.

Trivia: 4 Little Girls was nominated for the best feature documentary Oscar, and was seen as the clear favourite to win. However, a real shock occurred when Spike Lee and Sam Pollard lost out to Mark Jonathan Harris' Holocaust piece, *The Long Way Home* (1997).

Verdict: It's hard not to be moved by such a terrible story, and Spike gets the tone just right. 4/5.

8. The Triple Truth, Ruth

Although the phenomenon of *4 Little Girls* ultimately ended on a flat note with (perhaps predictable) Oscar disappointment, there was much for Spike and his fans to be thrilled about. For the first time since *Malcolm X*, Spike had produced a work that was receiving both good notices and widespread attention.

Although the documentary format is an area that Spike isn't primarily known for working in, the experience of directing *4 Little Girls* seemed to act as one where a massive pressure was taken off Spike's shoulders. Not just because of the success that the film enjoyed, but simply because he was working in a very different area of film. It's also highly possible that the grave subject matter reinforced the fact that some things are much more important than movies, much less how successful they are. *4 Little Girls* seemed to give Spike a real grounding at a key point in his filmmaking journey. The change of format, the difference in the way in which the film was released, and the emotional nature of the material all combined to blow the cobwebs away, and without this experience Spike probably wouldn't have gone on to make much more mature and organic works such as *He Got Game*, *Summer Of Sam* and *Bamboozled*. And let's not forget that, if Spike hadn't ventured down the road of exploring the Alabama church bombing, we wouldn't have had one outstanding documentary.

Anyway, the work that followed saw Spike shift into his third phase as a filmmaker (if parts one and two were separated by *Malcolm X*), and the films he went on to produce were the work of a far more mature director who seemed very much at home with his own technique.

He Got Game (1998)

Cast: Denzel Washington (Jake), Ray Allen (Jesus), Milla Jovovich (Dakota Burns), Ned Beatty (Warden Wyatt), Bill Nunn (Uncle Bubba), John Turturro (Billy Sunday), Jennifer Esposito (Ms Janus), Jim Brown (Spivey), Kim Director (Lynn), Chasey Lain (Buffy).

Crew: Writer/Director Spike Lee, Producers Jon Kilik & Spike Lee, Editor Barry Alexander Brown, Music Aaron Copland & Public Enemy, Production Designer Wynn Thomas, Cinematography Malik Hassan Sayeed, Costume Design Sandra Hernandez.

Story: Jake Shuttlesworth is a prisoner in Attica, where he's serving time for killing his wife. His son Jesus is one of the country's most promising basketball players, and on learning this the prison governor sees a way in which his old college - Big State - might gain a star player. The governor tells Jake that he'll reduce his sentence if he's able to persuade his son to sign up for Big State. He's prepared to release Jake for one week for this purpose, and sends him (and a pair of guards) to a Coney Island hotel. In the hotel Jake befriends prostitute Dakota Burns, and the two spend a night together.

Jesus wants nothing to do with his father, and we also learn that Jesus' coach, uncle and girlfriend all have selfish reasons for influencing the player's decision. Jake challenges his son to a one-on-one game of basketball; if Jake wins, Jesus will sign for Big State, but if Jesus wins Jake will leave his son's life forever. Jesus wins the game, and Jake returns to Attica. However, when the time to choose comes, Jesus decides on Big State. Back in prison, Jake is seen throwing a basketball over a wall, where it appears to be caught in a gym by a smiling Jesus.

Comment: With *He Got Game* Spike Lee returned to more familiar (non-documentary) territory, but his experience of making *4 Little Girls* seemed to have had a galvanising effect on him; not since *Clockers* had Lee shown the sort of hunger evident in *He Got Game*, and it stands up as being Lee's best collaboration with Denzel Washington.

He Got Game is essentially a fairly simple story, and one that echoes *Crooklyn* in both its setting (Brooklyn) and primary theme (the importance of family). Unlike *Crooklyn*, however, *He Got Game* has real structure and a driving narrative.

Out of all of Spike Lee's films, *He Got Game* is perhaps the most heartfelt and romantic. It's not sentimental to the point of becoming slushy, but it does have all the familiar ingredients of a Saturday night button-pusher - the jailed but essentially decent protagonist, the effectively orphaned kids, the faceless dollar men, the hooker with a heart of gold, and so on. For Spike Lee, it's dangerously by-the-numbers stuff, but his treatment of the material combined with Washington's performance makes the film into something far more than it should be.

As detailed earlier, sport has long been an interest (obsession?) of Lee's, and with *He Got Game* we see basketball play a major part in the story. In other Lee films sport has almost always figured purely as a reference point, or has served its purpose in helping spice up dialogue (think of Mookie and Vito's animated discussion about baseball in *Do The Right Thing*). However, in *He Got Game* we get a glimpse into Spike's own thoughts on the game of basketball. Forget about the 'metaphor for life' stuff that's often attached to sport in movies; in *He Got Game* it's clear that basketball possesses transcendental qualities. From the early shots of Jake playing ball in the prison courtyard to the scenes of Jesus practicing his game, it's clear that basketball is a means of rising above current problems, be they to do with imprisonment or trying to choose which college to attend. In some ways, this could be an analogy for black America - despite the historical problems that blacks have faced, it's largely African-Americans that built up and maintained professional basketball, a sport which has helped elevate the black community - just think of how many kids will have looked up to role models such as Michael Jordan and Shaquille O'Neal (both of whom, incidentally, appear as themselves in *He Got Game*). The almost spiritual quality of the game is amplified in the closing scene, where Jake throws the ball over the prison boundary where it's caught many miles away by his son. While this literally fantastic ending comes perilously close to over-egging the pudding that Spike's been expertly whipping up, it does at least provide an illustration of how Jake has finally managed to touch his son - with the help of basketball, of course.

As already mentioned, *He Got Game* emphasises the importance of family. The Shuttlesworth family, as seen in flashback, consists of a mother, father and two children. Like the Carmichaels in *Crooklyn*, they're an honest, ordinary lot who have the occasional problem - often centering around Jake's over-keenness to see the young Jesus work hard at his basketball. This unit is blown apart as a result of a heated argument where Jake pushes his wife aside, and she dies as a result of hitting her head awkwardly (by the way, how does Jake get put away for such a long stretch because of this? While he hardy deserved a medal, you'd think it would only be judged to be involuntary manslaughter). So, mum's dead, dad's jailed, and the kids are sent to stay with their aunt and uncle. This is where Spike's championing of the family unit becomes qualified, as it's obvious that this endorsement doesn't necessarily run to extended family. While they're initially seen to be kind to Jesus and his sister, the aunt and uncle - well, really Bubba, the uncle - emerge as having their own agenda. Bubba, aware of what a goldmine he's sitting on in the form of the ultra-talented Jesus, starts laying the guilt-trip on the young ball player. Bubba's intentions are barely masked - in a scene that references Francis Ford Coppola's *The Godfather Part II* (1974), he even states that he'd like to 'wet his beak' in all the riches that are headed Jesus' way. From this perspective, family proves to be no better than the myriad meddlers (the selfish coach, the duplicitous girlfriend, etc.) that litter Jesus' path. And while Jake may have his own reasons for influencing his son's choice of college, there can be little doubt that he cares immensely for his son. The only people who Jesus can really trust in the film are his sister and father - and he's not even aware of the latter's loyalty. *He Got Game*'s pretty big on the value of immediate family.

Although it often walks a fine line between the sublime and the ridiculous, *He Got Game* is easily one of Spike Lee's finest couple of hours. It's nicely photographed by Malik Hassan Sayeed, who wrings every drop of melancholy from the tarnished glitter of the Coney Island locations. Coney Island, with its legendary funfair and rides numbering the Cyclone and the now-dismantled Thunderbolt, is a haunting, ethereal part of Brooklyn, and since *He Got Game* was released it's been used in an equally (if not more) atmospheric manner in both Darren Aronofsky's *Requiem For A Dream* (2000) and Steven Spielberg's *AI: Artificial Intelligence* (2001). Somehow, it seems like a wholly appropriate backdrop to Jake's story - in many ways, both Jake and Coney Island are representative of faded dreams and a nostalgic yearning for brighter, better days.

He Got Game owes a lot to Denzel Washington's performance. There can't be many other actors of his generation that are this naturalistic, and as Jake he isn't afraid to look (and act) rough. In a lot of ways it isn't a flattering part, but Washington's playing of it makes it hard to take your eyes off him. Besides his performance, most of the other actors acquit themselves well: Ray Allen - who's not an actor at all but is actually a pro basketball player - does quite well as Jesus, *Crooklyn*'s Zelda Harris gives a winning performance as Jake's daughter, and Milla Jovovich is suitably sympathetic as the prostitute that Jake befriends.

By no means a perfect movie, *He Got Game* is perhaps Spike's only film that feels not particularly self-conscious. It's as if he's let himself off the leash to make an enjoyable and emotional movie, and the result is up there with the best films of the late 1990s.

Spike's Stock: He Got Game was Denzel Washington's third film for Spike; Bill Nunn went one better, clocking up his fourth appearance with the part of Uncle Bubba.

On the musical front Terence Blanchard got some rare time off, with Aaron Copland taking over composing duties.

Trivia: Porn star Chasey Lain plays one of the girls that 'welcomes' Jesus to a college hell-bent on landing his signature.

Verdict: He shoots, he scores: *He Got Game* is one out of the top drawer. Although at times a hard and gritty affair, there's a warm centre to this tale and Washington is at his best as likeable con Jake. Not one of Lee's most popular films, but definitely one of his most enjoyable. Great Public Enemy soundtrack, too. 5/5.

Summer Of Sam (1999)

Cast: John Leguizamo (Vinny), Mira Sorvino (Dionna), Jennifer Esposito (Ruby), Adrien Brody (Ritchie), Bebe Neuwirth (Gloria), John Savage (Simon), Patty Lupone (Helen), Anthony LaPaglia (Lou Petrocelli), Michael Badalucco (David Berkowitz), Ben Gazzara (Luigi), Spike Lee (John Jeffries), Kim Director (Dee).

Crew: Director Spike Lee, Writers Victor Colicchio & Michael Imperioli & Spike Lee, Producers Jon Kilik & Spike Lee, Editor Barry Alexander Brown, Music Terence Blanchard, Production Designer Therese DePrez, Cinematography Ellen Kuras, Costume Design Ruth E Carter.

Story: In the sweltering summer of 1977, New York City is in the process of being terrorised by a serial killer dubbed the Son of Sam. Bronx hairdresser Vinny appears to have few qualms about cheating on wife Dionna, but is given a scare when Sam kills a couple just next to where he was having sex with Dionna's cousin. Convinced that he's next on Sam's list, a nervous Vinny vows to mend his ways, although little actually changes. Meanwhile, Vinny's best friend Ritchie has become enamoured with the British punk scene that has begun to catch on in Manhattan, and his new clothes and attitude unnerve those that he grew up with in the Bronx.

As the summer heat gets worse and Sam's victim tally rises, the city is gripped by paranoia and hysteria. Ritchie and girlfriend Ruby immerse themselves in the punk band that they both play in, while Vinny and Dionna go for a night out which culminates in an orgy where Vinny becomes angry at his wife's behaviour. Dionna leaves Vinny, and the increasingly unhinged hairdresser also falls foul of his boss Gloria, with whom he's also enjoyed an affair. With Vinny's excitable friends starting to suspect that Ritchie may be the Son of Sam, a drug-addled Vinny finally stops trying to convince them otherwise and leads them to his best friend. The mob gives Ritchie a severe beating, but he's saved when his stepfather appears wielding a shotgun. The actual Son of Sam - real name David Berkowitz - is tracked to an address in Yonkers, and is led away by the police.

Comment: Summer ain't heaven in '77. Like *Do The Right Thing* from a full decade earlier, *Summer Of Sam* examines how the New York heat can drive people over the edge. Spike Lee has framed this tale in the apparently unoriginal format of a serial killer flick, although this proves to be a veneer that actually undersells the real value of the film by some considerable way.

The basic idea of essaying the exploits of a serial murderer is one that is by now extremely familiar; when Alfred Hitchcock's *Psycho* (1960) and Tobe Hooper's *The Texas Chain Saw Massacre* (1974) were released the whole concept seemed fairly innovative, but between those films and *Summer Of Sam*'s appearance in 1999 audiences had taken a bellyful of maniacal serial killer flicks which were of wildly varying quality: *Manhunter* (1986) and its sequels *The Silence Of The Lambs* (1991) and the ultra-lame *Hannibal* (2001), the Morgan Freeman movies *Se7en* (1995) and *Kiss The Girls* (1997), two sequels to *Psycho* (plus a prequel, a remake, and the bizarre TV movie *Bates Motel* (1987)), and three sequels to and a 25th anniversary re-release of *The Texas Chain Saw Massacre*. Even John McNaughton's superb *Henry: Portrait of a Serial Killer* (1986) suffered the ignominy of having a by-the-numbers sequel. Perhaps the sheer volume of such films is why *Summer Of Sam* performed fairly poorly at the box office (domestic gross: just over $19 million), and it's a pity that the rather unremarkable image of the film didn't attract viewers as *Sam* presented a remarkably intelligent and refreshing take on the sub-genre.

Taking its prompt from the flood of killings perpetrated by Yonkers resident David Berkowitz, *Summer Of Sam* sets out its stall early on in making it clear that this is what happened back in that sweaty summer of 1977. Lee doesn't skirt around the issues, or present events or people in an analogous or pseudonymous manner; the presence of New York tabloid journalist Jimmy Breslin (who, bizarrely, was considered for the role of Jimmy 'Popeye' Doyle in *The French Connection* (1971)) only reinforces the reality of the piece. Breslin received several highly-publicised letters from Berkowitz, and by having the journalist bookend the movie with his thoughts about 'Noo Yawk' it makes it nigh on impossible for the audience to get away from the fact that this film is about real events in a real city.

David 'Son of Sam' Berkowitz took a .44 and shot six people dead; a further seven were wounded as a result of his madness. This in itself is sensational enough, and the whole film could easily have focused on nothing besides these murders. Also, unlike fellow serial killers Charles Manson, Ted Bundy and Jeffrey Dahmer, the Berkowitz case has never really received that much in the way of ongoing publicity. Most people have heard of the Son of Sam, but a good deal fewer could actually tell you much about what he did. The details of the case haven't been overexposed, so you'd have thought that Lee would have been well within his rights to present us with nothing other than the story of David Berkowitz and his victims.

In what proves to be a remarkably gutsy and shrewd move, Lee decides to largely overlook the serial killer aspect and instead prefers to make Berkowitz merely one of many characters in the film. Although Berkowitz's activities are what put the city on the knife-edge, Lee is more interested in looking at how the inhabitants of the city behaved when under such pressure. In addition to the Sam killings, there were other factors that played their part in creating a pressure cooker atmosphere across the city - the extreme heat, the blackouts (and subsequent lootings), and the fact that the city's baseball team was on the verge of winning the World Series were all elements that conspired to wind this traditionally not-most-patient of cities up to ludicrous heights. With all this and more thrown into the melting pot, the Berkowitz killings are just one facet of the story, and Lee's interested in these murders because of the way in which they contributed to the bigger picture of what was happening across New York City.

Lee uses four main characters to tell the story of that fateful summer. There's hardworking waitress Dionna, her lecherous hairdresser husband Vinny, his best friend and punk aficionado Ritchie, and Ritchie's girlfriend Ruby. Things are more than a little fraught on most fronts, as besides everything else that's going on in the city each of the quartet have their own problems: Vinny and Dionna are having marriage problems (unsurprising, given his infidelities), while Ritchie and Ruby have both become alienated from the others in their neighbourhood on account of the couple's newfound interest in the punk movement that's been imported to New York from Britain. It probably wouldn't be so bad if the punk scene was happening in Ritchie's home patch of the Bronx, but that he and his girlfriend have to head over to Manhattan for the clubs that they like only contributes to the animosity that's stirring up in the direction of our Mohawk-sporting friend. The tight-knit Bronx community (which is ripe for accusations of stereotyping from those who've taken issue with Spike's depiction of Italian-Americans) come to the conclusion that Ritchie's the Son of Sam because he

74

dresses differently ('like a British fag,' as one of his so-called friends sneers), works at a strip club, and goads people in diners. These are the same clowns who consider that baseball star Reggie Jackson might be the killer as his number (44) is the same as the calibre of Sam's weapon of choice.

As already mentioned, the character of David Berkowitz isn't afforded too much in the way of screen time, and when we do see him it's either in his grungy apartment or putting his .44 to use in the streets of New York. The scenes in which Sam kills his victims are presented in a jarring, bloody manner - which is what you'd expect, given what the crimes involve. But, significantly, there's a real lack of sensationalism in these scenes, and Lee's filmed each killing in a near-documentary style - Ellen Kuras' camerawork adds to this quality - and the murders unfold in a manner which may shock or numb some viewers but never comes anywhere close to titillating. Lee executes these scenes in the same clinical manner as his subject does his victims, and it almost feels as if the director realises that he has to show these things, but would rather get them out of the way as quickly as he can so that he can return to his other characters. It also presents us with a refreshing and atypical viewpoint as far as screen multiple murderers are concerned; while many directors have been content to linger on scenes that show killers doing away with their victims, and indeed have often made these villains into loveable, cartoonish rogues, Lee is loathe to hand much of a platform to the murderer in his tale. Lee, it seems, realises that these people aren't witty or funny, and the way in which he skirts over Berkowitz shows that he's happy to deny these people the infamy they so desperately crave. No charming rascals like that good wine and fine art-loving culinary expert Hannibal Lecter can be found here.

It's been said that Lee awkwardly handled his predominantly white cast in this film, but this appears to be well wide of the mark. If Lee was less than confident when it came to working with these actors then he did a good job of hiding it, and the excellent commentary track that Spike recorded for the DVD release contains ample evidence of the affection and respect that he holds for the members of his large cast (*Sam* has over 100 speaking roles). In addition to the main four (John Leguizamo, Mira Sorvino, Adrien

Brody, Jennifer Esposito), the smaller roles are filled out by big performances from Bebe Neuwirth, Patti Lupone, Ben Gazzara, and John Savage.

Summer Of Sam should ultimately be viewed as not only a great thriller that wrings every drop of atmosphere from its New York locations, but also as a film that broke the mould on two counts: it reverted the serial killer to unfunny status, and also proved that a film could be made about the 1970s that didn't lapse into knowingly kitsch parody.

Spike's Stock: John Turturro became one of Spike's most-used actors by contributing the voice of Harvey the Dog, which took his tally of Lee films up to seven. Joie Lee went one better, making Sam her eighth film for her brother. Jennifer Esposito followed up her small role in *He Got Game* with an astonishing performance as Ruby, while John Savage marked the ten year anniversary of *Do The Right Thing* with a brief turn as sleazy Simon.

Behind the camera it was pretty much business as usual, although there was new blood in the form of production designer Therese DePrez.

Trivia: Summer Of Sam has no opening credits, although if you're not paying attention you may not notice. However, the letter blocks that David Berkowitz is fond of playing with actually spell out 'Son of Sam' at the start of the film.

Jennifer Esposito was originally down to play the role of Dionna, but scheduling difficulties led to her being re-cast as Ruby. In another Esposito-related twist, her grandmother lived on the same block as one of Sam's victims.

Sam was originally intended to be the directorial debut of Michael Imperioli, but in the end the *Sopranos* (1999) star settled for writing and acting credits. He wrote the script with his *Goodfellas/Sopranos* co-star Victor Colicchio before Lee contributed some work of his own.

Verdict: Spike in back-to-back classics shocker! After *He Got Game*, you'd have expected a bit of a disappointment, yet *Summer Of Sam* is arguably the finest film to bear the Lee signature. Scorsese would've been proud of this, and Tarantino can only dream of hitting such heights. 5/5.

The Original Kings Of Comedy (2000)

With: D.L. Hughley, Steve Harvey, Bernie Mac, Cedric the Entertainer.

Crew: Director Spike Lee, Producers David Gale & Walter Latham & Spike Lee, Executive Producer Van Toffler, Co-Producer Butch Robinson, Associate Producers Rylyn Demaris & Angelia Price, Editor Barry Alexander Brown, Production Designer Wynn Thomas, Cinematography Malik Hassan Sayeed, Art Director Tom Warren, Sound Rolf Pardula.

Story: A documentary capturing the performances of four esteemed stand-up comedians - D. L Hughley, Steve Harvey, Bernie Mac, and Cedric the Entertainer. Filmed over two nights in February 2000 in Charlotte, North Carolina.

Comment: Having flexed his documentary muscles with *4 Little Girls*, Spike returned to the format with this effort, which could hardly be further from the spirit of that chilling essay. Documenting the stage acts of four prominent black comedians, *Kings* is a work in which Lee shows his adeptness as a documentary filmmaker without (predictably) scaling the emotional heights of his previous foray into the format.

The Original Kings Of Comedy plays very much like an orthodox concert/performance film, and recalls two other films - *Eddie Murphy Raw* (1987) and *Richard Pryor Live On The Sunset Strip* (1982) - in its attempt to capture a significant moment in black comedy. To put the acts into some sort of context, the four comedians have all featured in US sitcoms, with Steve Harvey and Cedric the Entertainer co-starring in *The Steve Harvey Show* (1996). The Kings' live routine raked in around $37 million as it played for nearly 100 performances to packed houses across the US. This phenomenal success made it one of the biggest comedy shows for some time, and as such it was deemed to be worthy of documentation.

As is usually the case with Spike Lee films, *Kings* seems to exist for more than one reason. It can be enjoyed at face value as a riot of a comedy movie (depending on taste), but you also feel that Spike was well aware of how important this event was to black America. Therefore, it'd be a shame if all that was left once the show had run its course was anecdotal evidence concerning what the show was like, and by committing it to celluloid Spike was not only bringing the Kings' comedy to those people who couldn't get to the live shows, but was chronicling a time when black comedy made significant strides towards crossover appeal.

The huge success of *The Original Kings Of Comedy* (both the stage act and the film) provides a telling indication of the sort of thing that paying customers want to see - despite featuring all black players, *Kings* doesn't really engage with any real questions regarding race relations. There are a spattering of jokes highlighting the differences between blacks and whites, but no particularly pertinent points are made here. That may be stating the obvious seeing as *Kings* is a film of stand-up comedy, but comedy and social commentary needn't be mutually exclusive.

Of all of Spike's films, *The Original Kings Of Comedy* is second only to *Malcolm X* in terms of domestic box office takings. Grossing a whacking $38 million (marginally more than the live shows themselves), Lee had a huge hit on his hands. As much of the humour was US-specific, it wasn't as internationally saleable as many of Lee's other films, but it did provide him with some much-needed clout. It's ironic that a project that took a couple of days to film should dwarf the box office achievements of works such as *Clockers*, *Get On The Bus* and *He Got Game*, but it can at least be viewed as making some of the money that those films didn't and therefore evening things up somewhat. *The Original Kings Of Comedy* is slick, professional and clearly the work of a highly accomplished director, but it's without question inferior to Lee's best films.

Spike's Stock: Not many here. Barry Alexander Brown, Malik Hassan Sayeed and Wynn Thomas, but that's about it. Bernie Mac appeared as Jay in *Get On The Bus*.

Trivia: A film widely seen as a companion piece to *Kings* appeared shortly after the successful run of this film. *The Queens Of Comedy* (2001) was directed by Steve Purcell, and featured the stand-up routines of Laura Hayes, Adele Givens, Sommore, and Mo'Nique Imes-Jackson.

Verdict: With Spike at the helm you'd expect a solid documenary, and that's exactly what you get. Beyond that, it will all depend on whether you're a fan of the Kings' comedy or not. 3/5

Bamboozled (2000)

Cast: Damon Wayans (Pierre Delacroix), Jada Pinkett-Smith (Sloan Hopkins), Savion Glover (Manray/Mantan), Michael Rapaport (Dunwitty), Tommy Davidson (Womack/Sleep n' Eat), Thomas Jefferson Byrd (Honeycutt), Paul Mooney (Junebug), Kim Director (Starlet).

Crew: Writer/Director Spike Lee, Producers Jon Kilik & Spike Lee, Associate Producer Kisha Imani Cameron, Editor Sam Pollard, Music Terence Blanchard, Production Designer Victor Kempster, Cinematography Ellen Kuras, Costume Design Ruth E. Carter, Choreography Savion Glover.

Story: New York TV network executive Pierre Delacroix is under pressure to come up with a groundbreaking show. As the only black executive working at the network, Delacroix and his secretary Sloan devise the satirical *Mantan: The New Millennium Minstrel Show*, a highly offensive product that the exec is sure will soon come back to haunt the network. Delacroix gets two street performers, blackens up their faces, and changes their names from Manray and Womack to Mantan and Sleep n' Eat. The show consists largely of the duo acting like buffoons on a watermelon patch, while a band named The Alabama Porch Monkeys provide musical accompaniment.

Incredibly, the show is a runaway success, although it has its critics among the black community. Manray falls for Sloan, but things go badly wrong when the performer is abducted by militant rap artists Mau Mau - a group that includes Sloan's brother Julius. Mau Mau kill Manray, and the slaying is broadcast live on the Internet. As the group leave the site of the execution, the police gun them down. Devastated by the loss of both her brother and boyfriend, a hysterical Sloan shoots Delacroix dead.

Comment: Bamboozled is probably Spike Lee's most powerful film, and although it's by no means perfect it's a work that brilliantly manipulates the audience. Despite the uncomfortable laughs that are to be had at the expense of many of its larger than life characters, the film ultimately possesses a resonance that's rarely found in contemporary cinema.

The message is fairly hard to miss, as it basically concerns the ways in which film and television have stereotyped blacks. Although the minstrel show depicted in the film is really a product from another time, it is still perhaps no more than a couple of steps removed from some contemporary depictions of blacks; to leave the film thinking that Lee is simply attacking a now-defunct format would be to completely miss the point. *Mantan: The New Millennium Minstrel Show* may be far less subtle than the contemporary representations for which it is analogous, but Lee is saying that while actual productions like this may have ceased to exist there is still a similar mentality at work in some sections of the entertainment industry. When it comes to laying the blame, however, Lee doesn't see it as simply being a clear-cut case where whites have constructed these offensive caricatures; the director has publicly criticised the roles played by blacks in films as recent as *The Patriot* (2000) and *The Legend Of Bagger Vance* (2000) - the latter which ironically stars Will Smith, co-financer of Lee's *Get On The Bus* and husband of *Bamboozled* star Jada Pinkett. In *Bamboozled*, blacks are seen as being somewhat complicit in the perpetuation of these stereotypes. The two buskers that Pierre Delacroix uses in the show are initially seen to be pretty content to blacken up and play out the demeaning material as long as they are both performing and being handsomely paid for their efforts. Would-be militant rappers Mau Mau fare little better, with Lee painting them as being little more than vacuous sloganeers; their anger against *Mantan* seems to be derived more from failing an audition to appear on the show than it does from any objection to the actual content.

The title of the film is taken from a line in one of Malcolm X's speeches - 'You've been led astray, led amok, you've been bamboozled' - where the orator was trying to convey how blacks have been duped into playing second fiddle to the white man. In the film it's not too clear as to who's been doing the actual bamboozling, as it could be argued that both Delacroix and his gormless white boss Dunwitty are as much victims of unseen forces as both Manray and Womack. It almost seems as if present-day bamboozling occurs because of ingrained attitudes and not because people are consciously dreaming up racist material. These attitudes, of course, are a legacy from the executives who did contrive minstrel shows and similar.

Mantan: The New Millennium Minstrel Show is pretty hard to take, and both the racist imagery and the way in which it's lapped up by the studio audience are equally repellent. However, what is arguably the film's most disturbing moment occurs outside the confines of the show: Manray is shown burning corks over an alcohol solution and then applying the resultant black paste to his face in order to get the requisite blackened effect. As Terence Blanchard's score turns almost funereal, there's a haunted look in Savion Glover's eyes that makes this scene very hard to watch. It's one thing seeing Manray and Womack as African-Americans or even as blackened-up 'coons', but to watch one of them actually undergoing the undignified transformation is deeply upsetting; it's also a brilliant piece of acting by Glover. And although he's maybe not entirely blameless, it's hard not to feel some sympathy for the misguided Manray. His webcast execution is both disturbing as a spectacle and horrifying as a concept.

The only real criticism of *Bamboozled* is that it's occasionally overcooked. Invented TV commercials for alcoholic drink Da Bomb (replete with the catchphrase 'get your freak on') and 'Hillnigger' clothing tend to be so over the top that the danger is they'll only amuse audiences instead of making a perceptible point. In instances like these, less would have been more. Damon Wayans' performance is quite strange, too. Best known for his comedic roles, his portrayal of Delacroix is at once hammy and mesmerising. Sporting a weirdly clipped African-French accent, he initially appears to be little more than a caricature, although his descent into mental instability and a subplot involving his father add a bit more weight to the part.

Bamboozled was shot on Digital Video, and Ellen Kuras' cinematography makes the movie look pretty fantastic. The decision to use DV was partly due to the difficulties of funding the project, but if anything the occasionally fuzzy look only enhances the raw, vital edge of *Bamboozled* in a way that film could not. Having used DV for *The Original Kings Of Comedy*, *Bamboozled* proved that Lee could successfully employ the technology on a feature film. Interestingly, the *Mantan* sequences were shot on 16mm, a clever tactic, which goes a long way towards making the audience feel that the minstrel show is an actual programme that is being viewed from a DV-based reality.

Unfortunately, *Bamboozled* was not a commercial success. The difficulties in getting such a film funded appeared to apply to distribution as well, and the film was shown on less than 250 screens across the US. Putting *4 Little Girls* aside (which only got a very fleeting cinematic release, and in any case was made for HBO), *Bamboozled* is the lowest earner among Lee's domestic theatrical releases. The poor response is easily explained - *Bamboozled* is really not the sort of thing that most audiences would want to sit through on a Saturday night, and perhaps contains more hard truths than many viewers would be comfortable with.

Spike's Stock: New face Victor Kempster became the sixth production designer to have worked with Lee, but apart from that most of the crew had worked with Spike before. In addition to taking on the major role of Man-ray, Savion Glover choreographed the film.

Bamboozled was *Book Of Shadows: Blair Witch 2* (2000) star Kim Director's third film for Lee, and Denzel Washington can be glimpsed in inserted footage taken from *Malcolm X*.

Trivia: Although Damon Wayans and Jada Pinkett-Smith were both starring in their first film for the director, each had worked on films directed by Spike's old cinematographer Ernest Dickerson: Wayans on *Bulletproof* (1996), and Pinkett-Smith on *Demon Knight* (1995).

A favour for a favour? *Summer Of Sam*'s Mira Sorvino appears in *Bamboozled* as herself. Around the same time, Lee appeared as himself in the Sorvino-produced *Famous* (2000).

Verdict: A top-notch satire with real bite, *Bamboozled* might prove a bit strong for some but is rewarding viewing if you can stick it out to the bitter end. 4/5.

The 25th Hour (2002)

Cast: Edward Norton (Monty Brogan).

Crew: Producer/Director Spike Lee, Writer David Benioff, Producers Jon Kilik & Tobey Maguire & Nick Wechsler & Julia Chasman.

Story: Monty Brogan has been convicted of drug dealing offences. On the eve of starting his lengthy sentence, he spends time walking the New York streets with his girlfriend and his two closest friends. As the night wears on, Monty tries to trace back all the things that have happened, and attempts to pinpoint where it all went wrong. There are other influences at work, too: Monty's father thinks his son would be best to skip town, while his supplier wants to know if the young dealer has squealed.

Comment: As this book is being written Spike Lee's fifteenth theatrical feature is in pre-production. *The 25th Hour* is a low-budget adaptation of first-time author David Benioff's novel, and the finance and distribution for the film are being provided by the Walt Disney company (Disney offshoot Touchstone previously handled *He Got Game* for Spike).

Given that the rejuvenated, post-*4 Little Girls* Spike has yet to drop his game, *The 25th Hour* looks very promising. Lee and longtime colleague Jon Kilik are producing the film with the help of *Spider-Man* (2002) star Tobey Maguire, and the film stars Edward Norton, an actor who has proved to be arguably the finest actor of his generation with his turns in films such as *American History X* (1998) and *Fight Club* (1999).

The story itself sounds intriguing, and there are heavy echoes of *Clockers* in the subject matter: a young drug dealer faces the prospect of a jail term, while his supplier wants to know what he's told the police and the pusher's guardian has their own ideas about what their son should do. *The 25th Hour* should be more of a commercial success than *Clockers*, however, as it boasts a major box office star and has the weighty backing of Disney. It all sounds good, and hopefully won't lose anything in the translation from concept to screen...

9. Other Projects

Producing Credits

Spike Lee has served in some sort of producing role on every single one of his feature films, and he's used these skills to work on films outside of those that he's actually directed. All of these Lee-produced titles have come under the banner of his 40 Acres And A Mule Filmworks company, and it appears that Spike is extremely keen on giving first-time directors a leg up into the industry. Other than the films he's directed himself, Lee's producer credits are as follows.

Drop Squad (1994)

Cast: Eriq La Salle (Bruford), Ving Rhames (Garvey), Vondie Curtis-Hall (Rocky), Kasi Lemmons (June), Vanessa Williams (Mali).

Crew: Director David C Johnson, Writers David C Johnson & Butch Robinson, Producers Butch Robinson & Shelby Stone, Executive Producer Spike Lee, Music Mike Bearden, Cinematography Ken Kelsch, Editor Kevin Lee.

Comment: Drop Squad is a bit of a curio, chiefly because it stars a clutch of actors who've gone on to bigger things - Eriq La Salle has become virtually a household name with his role in TV's *ER*, while Ving Rhames gained a high profile with the likes of *Pulp Fiction* (1994) and the two *Mission Impossible* films (1996/2000). Vondie Curtis-Hall and Kasi Lemmons are both directors in their own right, although it's a profession that the former may have been sorry he entered into seeing as it's his name that's attached to the Mariah Carey über-bomb *Glitter* (2001).

Anyway, *Drop Squad*'s premise concerns a militant black group who abduct African-Americans that are deemed to have held back the race. The group is headed by Rhames and Curtis-Hall, and one of their main targets is advertising exec La Salle - a man behind tasteless campaigns as promoting fried chicken in packaging that displays the confederate flag. Once they get their man, they attempt to make him see the error of his ways, and try to impart just why what he's doing is so damaging.

Unfortunately, the premise doesn't get the treatment that it deserves, and *Drop Squad* ends up as a rather half-baked effort that doesn't really leave you with too much to think about. The ideas about a media exec who's lost touch with his background, and also the abduction of a fellow African-American by a militant group were to resurface in a far more effective manner in Lee's own *Bamboozled*.

New Jersey Drive (1995)

Cast: Christine Baranski (Prosecutor), Samantha Brown (Jackie), Gabriel Casseus (Midget), Sharron Corley (Jason), Devin Eggleston (Jamal), Conrad Meertins Jr (P-Nut).

Crew: Writer/Director Nick Gomez, Producers Bob Gosse & Larry Meistrich, Executive Producer Spike Lee, Co-Producer Rudd Simmons, Music Wendy Blackstone, Cinematography Adam Kimmel, Editor Tracy Granger.

Comment: A thought-provoking and impressively atmospheric work from director Nick Gomez, *New Jersey Drive* - as its title suggests - is set across the river from Spike Lee's home city of New York. The story centres on two black teenagers (Casseus and Corley) whose favourite pastime is joyriding. They're not the only ones in the area that indulge in such criminal activity, and things aren't quite as rosy when the police begin a major crackdown on car theft.

Way above average, *New Jersey Drive* kind of plays like a toned-down version of urban crime dramas such Lee's own *Clockers* and the Hughes Brothers' *Menace II Society* (1993). It isn't as relentlessly grim as either of those works, however, but is still a slow-burning tale that packs quite a hard punch. It's not the most widely seen film in recent times, but is well worth looking out for; the presence of the ever-excellent Christine Baranski (from TV's *Cybill* (1995) and the Jim Carrey blockbuster *The Grinch* (2000)) provides another good reason for giving this film a go.

Tales From The Hood (1995)

Cast: Clarence Williams III (Simms), Joe Torry (Stack), Samuel Monroe Jr (Bulldog), Wings Hauser (Strom), Michael Massee (Newton), Corbin Bernsen (Duke), Roger Guenveur Smith (Rhodie).

Crew: Director Rusty Cundieff, Writers Rusty Cundieff & Darin Scott, Producer Darin Scott, Executive Producer Spike Lee, Line Producer Elaine Dysinger, Music Christopher Young, Cinematography Anthony B. Richmond, Editor Charles Bornstein.

Comment: This is an anthology movie, which, as its name strongly implies, plays in a manner similar to fare such as *Tales From The Crypt* (1972) and *Twilight Zone: The Movie* (1983); incidentally, in the same year as this film Spike's erstwhile DoP Ernest Dickerson helmed the *Tales From The Crypt* movie *Demon Knight*.

The particular yarns that are spun here range from a heavy-handed tale involving racist cops to a more cerebral offering regarding the re-programming of a vicious gang member. Like many anthology movies that deal with the dark side, the results are at best patchy, and on the whole it's a fairly forgettable exercise. Dickerson's aforementioned *Demon Knight* is far from a masterpiece, but makes for a better evening's viewing than this sub-standard effort.

The Best Man (1999)

Cast: Taye Diggs (Harper), Nia Long (Jordan), Regina Hall (Candy), Jim Moody (Uncle Skeeter), Malcolm D Lee (Emcee).

Crew: Writer/Director Malcolm D. Lee, Producers Spike Lee & Sam Kitt & Bill Carraro, Music Stanley Clarke, Cinematography Frank Prinzi, Editor Cara Silverman.

Comment: This is a film that plays along similar lines to P. J. Hogan's *My Best Friend's Wedding* (1997): Harper is an author who goes to his best friend's wedding (where he's the best man), and meets a sort of old flame. Things get a little more complicated with the revelation that Harper once slept with the bride-to-be, and to top it all Harper has a girlfriend back home who he's in danger of losing unless he can untangle the whole mess.

The Best Man is quite nicely played, although there's nothing that new on display here. Taye Diggs proves a good choice for this sort of role, and he's given strong support from another *Ally McBeal* star - Regina Hall. For fans of twisty rom-coms, it'll go down a treat, but it's not the sort of film that'll really stick in the memory for too long. Still, after gritty urban drama and cod-horror, *The Best Man* at least proves that Spike isn't afraid to diversify when it comes to these projects. Oh, and in case you're wondering, director Malcolm D. Lee is a relation - cousin, to be exact.

Love And Basketball (2000)

Cast: Alfre Woodard (Camille), Regina Hall (Lena), Omar Epps (Quincy), Dennis Haysbert (Zeke), Debbi Morgan (Nona), Tyra Banks (Kyra).

Crew: Writer/Director Gina Prince-Bythewood, Producers Spike Lee & Sam Kitt, Executive Producers Jay Stern & Andrew Z Davis & Cynthia Guidry, Music Terence Blanchard, Cinematography Reynaldo Villalobos, Editor Terilyn A Shropshire.

Comment: After directing the excellent *He Got Game* Spike decided to take a back seat for this affecting tale in which the hallowed game of basketball is yet again at the forefront. The story centres on two youngsters - one girl, one boy - and their love of the game and each other. Both have ambitions to play in the NBA, and when college comes around they get together, split up, then after college get together again... or do they?

Love And Basketball is a very pleasant and highly watchable film. Director Gina Prince-Bythewood is the wife of writer Reggie Rock Bythewood, who penned Spike's *Get On The Bus*, and she does a really fine job in weaving this essentially tender tale that carries a few hard knocks along the way. The entire cast do well, particularly Lee's *Crooklyn* star Alfre Woodard, and *The Best Man*'s Regina Hall is also superb. It's not a powerhouse of a movie like *He Got Game*, but *Love And Basketball* certainly does both the game and the film's producer proud.

TV Work

Film is the format that's Spike's first love, and it's the medium in which he does the lion's share of his work. However, he has been known to delve into television - remember *4 Little Girls*' origins as an HBO film, although it became something far bigger than just another TV movie - and a few of the other occasions where he's dabbled in the small screen are detailed below.

Freak (1998)

With: John Leguizamo.

Crew: Director Spike Lee, Writers John Leguizamo & David Bar Katz, Executive Producers John Leguizamo & David Bar Katz & Robert Morton, Coordinating Producer Krysia Plonka.

Comment: John Leguizamo is an actor best known for his roles in films such as *Carlito's Way* (1993), *Moulin Rouge* (2001), *Ice Age* (2002) and of course Spike's own *Summer Of Sam*. However, *Freak* captures one of his greatest performances as it provides a document of the actor's stunning one-man stage show. During the course of the piece the audience are treated to numerous anecdotes concerning the Colombian-born star's upbringing, and it's not too clear which parts are true and what has been invented. The show is peppered with characters that the star has met along the way, and one particular standout moment has Leguizamo recalling how he worked with Lee Strasberg for a single day before the acting legend died. Leguizamo has a chameleon-like quality that makes his inhabiting of countless characters a real joy to watch, and the energy of his performance is very infectious. Deservingly, he picked up the award for Outstanding Performance in a Variety or Music Program at the 1999 Emmys. And if the show is this dynamic in the relatively distancing medium of television, just think what it must have been like to have been there.

A Huey P. Newton Story (2000)

Cast: Roger Guenveur Smith (Huey P Newton).

Crew: Director Spike Lee, Writer Roger Guenveur Smith, Producers Steven Adams & Bob L Johnson & Marc Henry Johnson, Editor Barry Alexander Brown, Cinematography Ellen Kuras, Production Designer Wynn Thomas, Music Marc Anthony Thompson, Sound Igor Nikolic.

Comment: After the huge success of *Freak*, Spike followed up that television work with another record of a one-man show. Capturing Roger Guenveur Smith's virtuoso performance, *A Huey P. Newton Story* was almost as dynamic a show as *Freak*, and works as ninety minutes of highly captivating entertainment.

Huey P. Newton was the co-founder of the Black Panther Party, and, like Malcolm X, was a complex character whose story has never really been fully told. The incredible off-Broadway show (that Roger Guenveur Smith also wrote) does a pretty good job of relaying a lot of the facets of this fascinating personality, and provides much in the way of valuable information as well as being entertainment in its own right. Roger Guenveur Smith has worked in minor roles on a number of Lee's films, but once you see him grab his chance to shine you'll wonder why on earth this guy isn't a household name. As photographed by the ever-reliable Ellen Kuras, *A Huey P. Newton* story goes far in staving off the cramped, stagy feel found in far too many one man shows. Like John Leguizamo in *Freak*, Roger Guenveur Smith's performance is huge, and in Lee he's found a director that can make a TV show a close second to actually catching the live performance.

3AM (2001)

Cast: Pam Grier (Georgia), Danny Glover (Hershey), Michelle Rodriguez (Salgado), Paul Calderon (Ralph), Mike Starr (Theo), Spike Lee (Filmmaker).

Crew: Writer/Director Lee Davis, Producer Spike Lee.

Comment: Lee Davis worked in minor technical roles (such as production assistant) on three consecutive Spike Lee films (*Mo' Better Blues*, *Jungle Fever* and *Malcolm X*), and with *3AM* he was granted his day in the sun, courtesy of a helping hand from his mentor.

The story follows a group of taxi drivers who spend time reflecting on love, life and the whole enchilada. Kind of like a heavier version of the now-defunct sitcom *Taxi* (1978), albeit one that's three times the length of one of the episodes of that classic show.

3AM was developed in conjunction with the Sundance Laboratory, and it's a film that feels very much like a first film: rough around the edges, but given some gravitas through the presence of seasoned performers including Danny Glover and the always impressive Pam Grier (players that are presumably drawing on native wit). Spike's guiding hand was obviously a big help to his protégé, and he presumably assisted in securing the presence a couple of actors (Paul Calderon, Mike Starr) who'd figured in his own directorial efforts. Not bad, if pretty much what you'd expect from a TV movie.

The Blues (2002)

With: Mya.

Crew: Directors Spike Lee & Wim Wenders & Leslie Harris & Charles Burnett & Mark Levin, Producer Margaret Bodde, Series Producer Alex Gibney, Executive Producer Martin Scorsese, Production Designer Liba Daniels.

Comment: This TV miniseries seems to have been 'in development' for quite a while; the title, and the presence of singing star Mya provide strong hints to the content of the programme, which will almost surely have a musical theme. With Lee's *Clockers* producer Martin Scorsese taking on executive producing duties and the co-directors including *Paris, Texas* (1984) helmer Wim Wenders, the show sounds like a halfway intriguing production.

10. Reference Materials

Videos & DVDs

Almost all of Spike Lee's films are available on video, and only a couple are currently unavailable on DVD. Of course, status of availability is always subject to change - new (and re) releases pop up from time to time, and items go out of print. Below is a guide to what's available, and where. Please note that I'm well aware that the world is made up of more than Europe and the US, but at least this shows where you might be able to pick up these films - either in the shops, or through online companies such as Amazon (.com, .co.uk & .de).

She's Gotta Have It (US VHS). Can be hard to find, but is the sort of tape that can be picked up from secondhand/auction sites such as Ebay or Amazon's Marketplace/ZShops.

School Daze (US VHS, Region 1 DVD).

Do The Right Thing (US & Europe VHS, Region 1 & 2 DVD). Besides the standard one disc edition, there's a special double disc available that's been put together by the Criterion company. As well as commentary by Spike Lee, Joie Lee, Wynn Thomas and Ernest Dickerson, this package includes a whole disc of supplementary material: *The Making Of Do The Right Thing* (an hour-long documentary), Public Enemy's *Fight The Power* music video, the press conference from Cannes '89, a trailer, storyboards, and more. The film itself looks and sounds great in this transfer, and this package is the only option for hardcore fans of the film and/ or director.

Mo' Better Blues (US & Europe VHS, Region 1 DVD)

Jungle Fever (US & Europe VHS, Region 1 & 2 DVD)

Malcolm X (US & Europe VHS, Region 1 & 2 DVD)

Crooklyn (US VHS, Region 1 DVD)

Clockers (US & Europe VHS, Region 1 & 2 DVD)

Girl 6 (US & Europe VHS)

Get On The Bus (US VHS, Region 1 DVD)

4 Little Girls (US & Europe VHS, Region 1 DVD)

He Got Game (US & Europe VHS, Region 1 DVD). The DVD apparently has little in the way of extra features (just a trailer), but the US VHS contains the music video for Public Enemy's *He Got Game*, which is a nice bonus.

Summer Of Sam (US & Europe VHS, Region 1 & 2 DVD)

The Original Kings Of Comedy (US VHS, Region 1 DVD). There's also a region 1 DVD gift pack available, which features *The Original Kings Of Comedy* and its 'sister' film *The Queens Of Comedy*.

Bamboozled (US & Europe VHS, Region 1 & 2 DVD)

In addition to the above, there's also a region 2 DVD box set available, which contains *Do The Right Thing*, *Jungle Fever* and *Clockers*. A region 1 triple set also exists, consisting of *Mo' Better Blues*, *Jungle Fever* and *Crooklyn*.

Soundtracks

The soundtracks to most of Spike's films can be bought on CD; the list below denotes those currently available.

School Daze. A compilation of tracks from the film, including the infamous *Straight And Nappy*.

Do The Right Thing. An excellent Bill Lee score, but note that this album doesn't include Public Enemy's *Fight The Power*. For that track, check out the band's *Fear Of A Black Planet*

Mo' Better Blues. Doesn't feature John Coltrane's *A Love Supreme*, despite the tracks prominence in the film.

Jungle Fever. Stevie Wonder's songs from the film.

Malcolm X. Two different albums available - Terence Blanchard's excellent score, plus a classy soundtrack album featuring the likes of Billie Holliday, Ray Charles, Ella Fitzgerald and John Coltrane.

Crooklyn. Two separate volumes available.

Clockers. Features tracks from Chaka Khan, Des'ree, Seal, etc.

Girl 6. A must for Prince fans (and the album's actually credited to Prince as opposed to that funny symbol thingy), this soundtrack features then-new tracks plus songs from the purple one's vaults, such as *Girls And Boys* and *The Cross*.

Get On The Bus. This is one of those 'music from and inspired by...' soundtracks. It's not an album of Terence Blanchard's music, but rather is a compilation of tracks by artists including Curtis Mayfield, Stevie Wonder, and Earth Wind and Fire.

He Got Game. Two different albums available - one contains Aaron Copland's score, while the other is a collection of Public Enemy's songs from the film (further still, this album is available in both 'clean' and 'explicit' versions).

Summer Of Sam. Contains '70s tracks from Abba, Chic, etc., along with The Who's *Baba O'Riley*. Please note that this is the only Who track on the album - those wanting a bit more (including *Won't Get Fooled Again*, which also features in the film) should seek out the band's album *Who's Next*.

The Original Kings Of Comedy. Contains music, plus some of the Kings' stand-up material.

Bamboozled. Includes Bruce Hornsby's *Shadowlands*, among other tracks.

Books

There are quite a few books on Spike Lee and his work; as always, these can both come in and go out of print at short notice, but the advent of the internet has made the tracking down of out of print books a much easier task. Here's a few that you should be able to get your hands on. I haven't read all of these, so please don't take this list as an unreserved endorsement of each and every one of these titles...

Five For Five: The Films Of Spike Lee by David Lee and Spike Lee, 1991 Stewart, Tabori & Chang; ISBN: 1556702175. Interesting book that acts as a photographic record of Spike's first five feature films. Includes an introduction by Spike himself.

By Any Means Necessary: The Trials And Tribulations Of The Making Of Malcolm X by Spike Lee & Ralph Wiley, 1992 Hyperion; ISBN: 1562829130. Not to be confused with the similarly-titled Jim Haskins book, this book is a quite superb record of the struggle that Lee and his team had on their hands while filming *Malcolm X*. It's an essential purchase for all Lee fans, and includes the screenplay to boot.

Spike Lee: Filmmaker by Bob Bernotas, 1993 Enslow Publishers; ISBN: 0894904167. Published around the time of *Malcolm X*'s release, the title actually undersells the book as in here you'll find biographical info on Spike's childhood, before following through to his work on films up to and including *Malcolm X*.

Spike Lee: Filmmaker by James Earl Hardy & Nathan Irvin Huggins, 1994 Chelsea House Publications; ISBN: 079101875X. Not to be confused with the Bob Bernotas book mentioned above, this is part of the *Black Americans Of Achievement* series, and is a useful educational work - particularly suitable for younger teens.

Best Seat In The House by Spike Lee & Ralph Wiley, 1997 Fourth Estate; ISBN: 1857027876. This book doesn't have that much to do with Spike's films, but instead is a basketball memoir that details its co-authors obsession with the New York Knicks. A good read, although only of interest to serious fans of Spike and/or the game.

Spike Lee: By Any Means Necessary by Jim Haskins, 1997 Walker & Company; ISBN: 0802784968. Prolific author Jim (AKA James) Haskins has turned out over one hundred books, many of them biographies dealing with prominent African-Americans. Here he takes a look at Spike's life and work, and his assured writing style makes for a pleasant, undemanding read.

Spike Lee's Do The Right Thing by Mark A. Reid (Editor), 1997 Cambridge University Press; ISBN: 0521559545. A collection of essays on the film, all of which are fairly detailed. The essays look at various aspects of the film, such as the music, the use of New York, and so on. It also tries to place the action that takes place in *Do The Right Thing* in the context of racial problems across the US, and also contains a decent range of production stills.

Spike Lee: On His Own Terms by Melissa McDaniel, 1998 Franklin Watts; ISBN: 0531114600. Like *Spike Lee: Filmmaker*, this title is a useful teaching resource that's best suited to younger secondary (or older primary) schoolchildren.

Spike Lee: Interviews by Spike Lee & Cynthia Fuchs, 2002 University Press of Mississippi; ISBN: 1578064708. Does what it says on the tin, really: a book of interviews with a man who's never been scared to voice his opinion.

World Wide Web

There's a real lack of comprehensive Spike Lee sites, and the web is crying out for someone to have a go at creating a one-stop shop for fans of the director. The sites/pages below will give you some info on Spike, his work and some related areas, but no single one of them could be described as definitive.

http://www.4littlegirls.com - Excellent site concerning the Birmingham, Alabama church bombing. Lots of info on the investigations, and a fine resource for those who want to learn more about this terrible case.

http://www.ahueypnewtonstory.com - For those that enjoyed Spike's TV version of this play, this site takes the screen version as its starting point to introduce you to a lot more about Black Panther co-founder Huey P. Newton.

http://www.bamboozledmovie.com - Nicely designed site about *Bamboozled*. Includes cast and crew bios, production info, etc.

http://www.kingsofcomedymovie.com - Site for the highly successful film (and stage act).

http://www.salon.com/10/reviews/spike1.html - This section of the excellent Salon site contains a detailed analysis of *Girl 6*, and also casts the net a bit wider as it looks as Spike's role as a black filmmaker.

http://www.terenceblanchard.com - A page devoted to the composer for much of Spike's work, including info on his solo stuff and other activities.

http://timecast1.timecast.com/spikelee/theater/leebio_frm.html - Quite a nice (if somewhat dated) little page, with a bio, 'jointography' and a theatre area.

http://www.upcomingmovies.com/summerofsam.html - The title of this site gives a big clue to the fact that this info is hardly current. Nonetheless, it contains some interesting information on *Summer Of Sam*.

The Essential Library: Currently Available

Film Directors:

Woody Allen (2nd)	Tim Burton	Ang Lee
Jane Campion*	John Carpenter	Joel & Ethan Coen (2nd)
Jackie Chan	Steven Soderbergh	Clint Eastwood
David Cronenberg	Terry Gilliam*	Michael Mann
Alfred Hitchcock (2nd)	Krzysztof Kieslowski*	Roman Polanski
Stanley Kubrick (2nd)	Sergio Leone	Oliver Stone
David Lynch	Brian De Palma*	George Lucas
Sam Peckinpah*	Ridley Scott (2nd)	James Cameron
Orson Welles (2nd)	Billy Wilder	Roger Corman
Steven Spielberg	Mike Hodges	Spike Lee

Film Genres:

Blaxploitation Films	Bollywood	French New Wave
Horror Films	Spaghetti Westerns	Vietnam War Movies
Slasher Movies	Film Noir	Hammer Films
Vampire Films*	Heroic Bloodshed*	Carry On Films
German Expressionist Films		

Film Subjects:

Laurel & Hardy	Marx Brothers	Film Music
Steve McQueen*	Marilyn Monroe	The Oscars® (2nd)
Filming On A Microbudget	Bruce Lee	Writing A Screenplay
Film Studies		

Music:

The Madchester Scene	Beastie Boys	Jethro Tull
How To Succeed In The Music Business		

Literature:

Cyberpunk	Philip K Dick	The Beat Generation
Agatha Christie	Sherlock Holmes	Noir Fiction*
Terry Pratchett	Hitchhiker's Guide (2nd)	Alan Moore
William Shakespeare	Creative Writing	Tintin

Ideas:

Conspiracy Theories	Nietzsche	UFOs
Feminism	Freud & Psychoanalysis	Bisexuality

History:

Alchemy & Alchemists	The Crusades	The Black Death
Jack The Ripper	The Rise Of New Labour	Ancient Greece
American Civil War	American Indian Wars	Witchcraft
Globalisation	Who Shot JFK?	

Miscellaneous:

Stock Market Essentials	How To Succeed As A Sports Agent	Doctor Who

Available at bookstores or send a cheque (payable to 'Oldcastle Books') to: **Pocket Essentials (Dept SL), P O Box 394, Harpenden, Herts, AL5 1XJ, UK.** £3.99 each (£2.99 if marked with an *). For each book add 50p(UK)/£1 (elsewhere) postage & packing